THE
SEARCH
FOR
JEWISH
THEOLOGY

THE SEARCH FOR JEWISH THEOLOGY

by

BERNARD J. BAMBERGER

Behrman House, Inc.
Publishers
New York

Library of Congress Cataloging in Publication Data

Bamberger, Bernard Jacob, 1904–
    The search for Jewish theology.

    Includes bibliographical references.
    1. Jewish theology.   I. Title.
BM601.B33   296.3   77–28457
ISBN 0–87441–300–1

Published by Behrman House, Inc.
1261 Broadway, New York, N.Y. 10001
Manufactured in the United States of America

83   82   81   80   79   78

10   9   8   7   6   5   4   3   2   1

To
Our
Children

CONTENTS

We ask of Theology to express that element in perishing lives which is undying by reason of its expression of perfections proper to our finite natures. In this way we shall understand how life includes a mode of satisfaction deeper than joy or sorrow.

Alfred North Whitehead

THE
SEARCH
FOR
JEWISH
THEOLOGY

Chapter I

AN APPROACH TO RELIGIOUS THINKING

The Theological Animal. The ancient Greeks defined man as a "rational animal." In the medieval Hebrew version of this classification, the term *speaking* was substituted for *rational*. No irony was intended; speech was regarded as evidence of man's rationality.

Still, the change is suggestive, for though many people avoid the stress and fatigue of hard thinking, most of us are subject to a strong urge to talk. This need for speech is generated especially by intense and unusual experiences for which words cannot readily be found. Hence the continuing popularity of love songs.

So it is, too, with the experiences we call religious, which we may tentatively describe as the experiences concerned with life's highest values. One who has had such an experience—ritual, mystical, ethical—feels the need to talk about it, to try to make clear to himself what has happened to him, and to convey to others something of the wonder it brought. The attempt to find words for religious experience is what we mean initially by the word "theology."

Since religion is a virtually universal human phenomenon, we might even define man as the theological animal, the being who not only must talk, but must talk sometimes about the divine.

• **Systematic Theology.** The theologian tries to make the religious experience articulate in words. But in addition, he often

1

tries to organize the disconnected fragments of such experience into an orderly whole. The experience may be his own. More often, however, he works with sacred writings and traditions which record the visions, intuitions, and inner struggles of others, whom he regards as specially inspired. But such primary data, whether firsthand or not, are incomplete and unclear. The theologian tries to determine their meaning and their implications, to arrange them into a consistent pattern, to iron out apparent contradictions, to fill in gaps, and then to extend the principles he has elicited so that he may deal securely with problems and questions which the sacred documents do not plainly discuss.

Often he must go further and take into account the scientific and philosophic thought of his own time. He may want to show that his religious doctrine is in basic agreement with the dominant outlook of the age—perhaps modifying one or both elements in order to make them fit together. Or he may use a current philosophy as the framework for his theological construction. Should he find his faith incompatible with the predominant thinking of the time, he may find it necessary to give a reasoned argument for rejecting that predominant view.

This entire enterprise is summed up in the term *systematic theology.*

● **Unsystematic Judaism.** From Bible times on, the Jews produced a voluminous literature. But remarkably, no systematic presentation of Jewish religious beliefs was attempted until the tenth century C.E., when the religion of Israel had been in existence for some two thousand years! Even then, this happened in response to a challenge from without. Arab scholars had rediscovered and disseminated the philosophic ideas of ancient Greece, and these ideas had unsettled the minds of many believers. And therefore the greatest Jewish leader of the period, Rav Saadia Gaon, found it necessary to compose a reasoned exposition of Jewish doctrine, the *Book of Beliefs and Opinions.*[1]

Until then, the need for such a formulation had seldom been felt. Yet Judaism before Saadia was neither primitive, naive, nor isolationist. The Jewish intellectuals of earlier centuries had been well aware of Greek pagan philosophy and of Christian theology. They chose not to cultivate these disciplines and apply them to the exposition of Jewish beliefs, for reasons we can only surmise. But consciously or unconsciously, they were expressing the genius of Judaism, employing a method and style different from that of systematic theology. It is an approach that might *almost* be called experimental.

• **The Way of Experiment.**   Contemporary science differs from that of Aristotle not only in the greater bulk and exactness of its data, but in fundamental method as well. Aristotle sought to construct, especially in physics, a system whose correctness would be guaranteed by its logical consistency. A number of first principles were set up, based on limited and largely untested data; and then conclusions were drawn fron them by deductive logic.

In contrast, the modern scientist accepts no conclusion as valid, no matter how logically compelling it seems, until he has tested it by means of controlled experiment.

Systematic theology was for a long time dominated by Aristotelian methods. Even after the decline of medieval scholasticism, Christian thinkers still ascribed great importance to logical consistency. There is no more remorseless application of this principle than John Calvin's *Institutes of the Christian Religion.*

But another method of theologizing is possible. It would examine every theological proposition and test it by reference to all the realities of human life. The theologian's task would then become one of exploration rather than organization. With such an approach, the validity of an affirmation is not necessarily destroyed because it cannot be fitted neatly into an all-embracing scheme.

Physicists currently operate with two contrasting theories on the nature of light. This procedure is intolerable when judged by Aristotle's principle of contradiction: light cannot be at one and the same time a stream of corpuscles and a series of waves. The contemporary scientist is surely not happy about this situation; he would much prefer a single hypothesis that would explain all the phenomena of light. But for the present, he finds both theories useful; he would rather work with both than ignore or distort data in order to force everything into one pattern.

In somewhat similar fashion, we should be prepared to take into account all the data of religious experience, from all possible sources, and examine them carefully, even though we may not be able to organize them into a single consistent whole.

This "experimental" approach to religious thought, however, is only in a limited degree analogous to the experimental method of modern science. The data of religion do not lend themselves to controlled, repeatable experiment. (This is also true of some areas of natural science and of many areas of the social sciences.) The claim made some years ago by certain Protestant thinkers that theology is, or can become, an empirical science appears to be a wild overstatement.[2] The best description of our method is "exploratory."

• **Rationalism and Rationality.**   This is in no sense a defense of irrationality. Logic may not be an absolute, but to shrug off its demands would be irresponsible. A foolish consistency may be, in Emerson's phrase, "the hobgoblin of little minds"; but one does not show himself to be a great mind by the simple practice of inconsistency. The physicist may be obliged to operate with two theories of light, but he doesn't glory in that fact. Paradox is a reality with which we must wrestle, not a badge of superiority to be worn with ostentation.

Our approach is intended to be rational, but not rationalistic.

Rationalism generally implies the confidence that human reason can solve all the problems, theoretical and practical, that need to be solved. The more cautious rationalists do not indeed claim to have solved all problems, though they often come close to such an assertion—where does Spinoza, for example, refer to a question that requires further study?—but they seem to suggest that a little more digging, a little more refinement of method will fill in the remaining gaps in our knowledge.

In practice, rationalists have often resorted to dubious means of completing their systems and keeping them consistent— forced arguments, distorted evidence, and disregard for or minimizing of inconvenient facts.

True rationality appears to me both more humble and more painful. More humble, because it recognizes that the potential of reason, though vast, is not unlimited, and that there are areas of significant human experience that do not readily lend themselves to rational treatment. More painful, because it finds itself confronted with contradictions and discrepancies from which it cannot escape. It isn't easy to live with such a situation. We are tempted to resort to some reductionist device, or to a verbal trick that makes all difficulties disappear. Or we may call reason bad names and retreat into some form of irrationality. The honest policy is to do none of these things, but to keep on applying our intelligence to the problems before us—even if we get no further than the discovery that logically we are in trouble. There is no better exercise in rationality than the admission that we have tackled a problem and have not succeeded in solving it.

• **Theology and Philosophy.**   Once regarded as the "queen of sciences," theology has been widely denigrated in the last two or three centuries. More recently, the intellectual world has been showing greater respect for theology and theologians. We need not inquire here into the reasons for these changes of fashion. But it is proper to note the substantial difference between theology and philosophy, even philosophy of religion. Theology is the expression of a commitment made in advance. The theologian articulates and explicates his faith and experience. Philosophy is supposed to be an objective inquiry, begun without preconceptions. Thus a philosopher of religion may analyze fairly and sympathetically religious doctrines which he himself does not accept. The theologian's business is to expound what he believes.

This does not preclude his use of rigorous method. His presentation may be learned, profound, and tightly reasoned; it may surpass in these respects much that passes under the name of philosophy. In fact, the theologian may have an advantage in that he knows he is partisan. The philosopher may not so readily recognize his own preoccupations, prejudices, and assumptions, especially if they are the generally accepted preconceptions of his time.

Among ancient thinkers there was a widespread opinion that

the philosopher ought to be impassive. In contrast, some moderns insist that we ought to philosophize with passion.[3] Certainly theology, rooted as it is in conviction, ought not be too relaxed and prosy. But we must beware of measuring the intenseness of passion by the quality of literary style. Kant was just as passionate a philosopher as Nietzsche, though the latter wrote with poetry and wit, and the former in a crabbed and pedantic manner. One cannot judge the depth and strength of a person's convictions by the loudness of his voice.

THE APPROACH IN FORMER TIMES

There can be no doubt that prior to the Middle Ages, Jewish religious teachers dealt with problems of belief in an unsystematic, fluid, and exploratory fashion. It was their example, chiefly, that suggested that a return to their classic style may be profitable even today. Such a return cannot, of course, be a slavish imitation. But before we consider how their method may be adapted to our circumstances and needs, it will be helpful to take a closer look at that classic style in the classic sources, Bible and Talmud.

• **Philosophy in the Bible.**   There is no consistent theological system running through the Bible. A collection of writings in prose and poetry, composed by many authors over a space of nearly a thousand years, cannot be a homogeneous and ordered whole. But even in individual writings we find little of that discursive reasoning, that organization of abstractions, which came to the world through the Greeks and which they named "philosophy." The biblical authors stress the concrete and the individual rather than the general; they are more concerned with deed than with concept; they engage in passionate affirmation and negation rather than in detached, objective contemplation.

Yet the Bible contains many passages which display a speculative profundity that can only be called philosophic.

Individual insights rather than extended expositions, they are all the more impressive because of their simple brevity.

The informed reader may think of the book of Ecclesiastes, with its thoroughgoing skepticism, and of the book of Job, which dissents from orthodoxy in a more affirmative way.[4] But even more conventional contexts provide examples of philosophic depth.

We need go no further than the first chapter of Genesis, that orderly account of creation by divine fiat, so different in tone from the more colorful and "mythical" creation story in the second chapter. Actually, the first chapter also derives from ancient myth, preserved in writings from Mesopotamia, but here that myth has been transmuted into something almost scientific in tone.

Particularly significant is the use of the word "create" (in Hebrew, *bara*), a verb reserved in the Bible for the creative acts of God. The usual Hebrew words for "make," "do," "shape," "act," and so on are also used of God, but *bara* is never used of man. So strongly was this felt that even in modern Hebrew, which has secularized a good many ancient sacred terms, the verb *bara* and its derivatives are never applied to a "creative" artist and his works. This special word does not apparently refer to "creation out of nothing"—a very difficult concept—but to the uniqueness of God's activity. It implies what the words of the prophet make explicit: "My plans are not your plans, nor are My ways your ways" (Isaiah 55:8). This same prophet repeatedly stresses the uniqueness, the incomparability of God: "To whom, then, can you liken Me, to whom can I be compared?—says the Holy One. Lift high your eyes and see: Who created these? (Isaiah 40:25-26).

These insights are not obvious. An ancient Hittite document containing instructions for sacrifice asks, "Are the minds of men and of the gods generally different?" and replies, "No! With regard to the matter with which they are dealing? No! Their minds are exactly alike."[5] The Israelite prophets lived many centuries after this Hittite text was written, but we have very little evidence that the intellectual and spiritual advances found in the Bible were paralleled among the other Near Eastern peoples.

As some biblical authors thought profoundly about God, so they also thought profoundly about man. Here again we start with the first chapter of Genesis, which declares that God created man in His image. This statement cannot mean that man is physically a smaller replica of God—the entire chapter has an abstract, almost scientific tone; rather it asserts the worth of man as somehow akin to the Creator. What is said here simply and soberly takes fire in the eighth Psalm:

> When I behold Your heavens, the work of Your fingers,
> The moon and stars that You set in place:
> What is man that You have been mindful of him,
> Mortal man that You have taken note of him,
> That You have made him little less than divine,
> And adorned him with glory and majesty!

The dignity of man within creation, and his littleness in comparison with the unique God, could not be stated more powerfully. In form and style this is not philosophy, in depth of insight it can hardly be called anything else.

• **Abraham Argues with God.**   The Bible, then, contains not only vivid narrative and passionate poetry, but speculative elements as well. We may now consider some instances of exploratory thinking.

Reading the tale of Abraham's plea for the people of Sodom (Genesis 18:22 ff.), we are struck at once by the repeated efforts of the patriarch to get a reduction in the minimum number of righteous persons needed to save the city. People sometimes speak of Abraham's haggling with God, but that is not correct. Abraham has no bargaining power; he simply pleads with the Deity. But this series of pleadings serves only to underscore the central thought of the story: "Shall not the Judge of all the earth deal justly?"

In view of the remarks frequently made about the harsh, unrelenting justice of the "Old Testament," it is instructive to note the concept of justice in this passage. The author holds that it would be unjust for even a small handful of good people to perish along with the wicked majority; he does not worry that the escape of a wicked majority through the merits of a righteous few might also be a miscarriage of justice.

The story is, in fact, a sort of trial run for the idea of what is now called vicarious atonement. The writer seems to be struggling with the notion, and we are not sure what conclusion he arrives at. Even though Abraham obtains the assurance that the city will be spared if it contains ten righteous persons, destruction follows swiftly. Apparently ten righteous men could not be found.

But the idea of vicarious atonement persists in biblical thought. It could hardly be otherwise; for, however we judge it as a doctrine, it derives from realities that can be observed. For example: We, the heirs of an ancient civilization, benefit by the accumulated experience and wisdom, as well as by the mistakes and frustrations, of our predecessors. Our own shaky virtue is fortified by the instruction, and still more the example, of our parents and teachers. Even the good reputation of our forebears benefits us materially and spiritually. And the suffering endured for a compelling cause generates added loyalty to that cause.

And so, not surprisingly, the Bible stresses the great righteousness of the patriarchs, which redounded to the benefit of their descendants. Israel was chosen by God, redeemed from Egypt, and given the land flowing with milk and honey because of the merits of their ancestors; for the sake of Abraham, Isaac, and Jacob, God saved their children—and will save them—from the destruction they deserved because of their own sins.

This concept of "the merit of the fathers" holds an important place in Talmudic thought as well. But neither in Bible or Talmud is the thought hardened into dogma. The principle of the merit of the fathers is not permitted to negate the freedom of God to punish or forgive; nor is it allowed to overshadow the thought that each generation has its own moral responsibility.*

---

*The converse proposition, that children suffer for the sins of their parents, is also found occasionally; because it is included in the Ten Commandments (Exodus 20:5), more attention has been given it than it would otherwise have received. The principle was rejected regarding

The most famous utterances in the Bible about vicarious atonement are those regarding the "suffering servant of the Lord" (Isaiah 42, 49, 50, 53). These passages were to serve as a primary source for the Christian doctrine of the Atonement. Still today scholars disagree on the identity of the servant: did the writer have in mind an actual prophet, the expected Messiah, or simply the people of Israel personified? We need not enter into that tangled discussion. For it is clear, in any case, that the sufferings of the servant have a redemptive power for others. Future generations will say of him:

> He bore the chastisement that made us whole,
> And by his bruises we were healed. (Isaiah 53:5)

Yet, despite many references to the notion in Scripture and later Jewish literature, vicarious atonement did not become a dogma in Judaism, as it did in Christianity.

● **"Hallowed Be Thy Name."** Another instance of the exploratory approach begins with Ezekiel, the prophet of the Babylonian exile. In contrast to most of the biblical authors, Ezekiel was inclined to a somewhat doctrinaire way of thinking. He agreed with the prophets before him, and those who came later, that the fall of the kingdom of Judah and the exile to Babylon were a fully deserved punishment for the sins of the nation. Indeed, strict justice would have required the complete annihilation of the people.

Now in ancient times the defeat of a nation was regarded as the defeat of its national god or gods; the gods of the victors were obviously stronger. So when the people of Judah were conquered and exiled, the reputation of their God suffered accordingly—in Ezekiel's language, "His name was profaned among the nations." It was necessary for Him then to retrieve

---

human criminal justice (Deuteronomy 24:16) and was repudiated as a theological concept by Ezekiel (see pp. 11–12). But even in the Ten Commandments the statement has a paradoxical character: the divine punishment extends only to the third and fourth generations of the offender, whereas mercy continues to the thousandth generation of the righteous. Plainly, these judgments are not the fruit of abstract logic.

His reputation, to "sanctify His name," by showing that the exile was due, not to His weakness, but to His unswerving justice. This could be accomplished only if His people were restored to their land and granted prosperity and power. That they might be worthy of this redemption, Ezekiel declared, God Himself would bring about their spiritual regeneration (Ezekiel 36:16 ff.).

Another prophet of the period recast this notion both in intent and language. God would indeed bring about the redemption of His people, even though they did not deserve it.

> It is I, I, who—for My own own sake—
> Wipe your transgressions away
> And remember your sins no more. (Isaiah 43:25)

God will act, not chiefly to improve His public image, but because it is His nature to rescue and regenerate.[6]

The terminology of Ezekiel survived in the consciousness of the people, but its force was completely transformed in Talmudic times. A highly dubious theological concept was recast into a powerful moral challenge. Every Jew, it was taught, has a responsibility to uphold God's reputation. Any action that brings discredit on Jews and Judaism is a profanation of the name of God; every act of dignity, rectitude, and generosity serves to sanctify the name. The familiar words "Hallowed be Thy name" do not mean "Holy is Thy name," but rather "May our conduct bring new luster to the name of the God we worship." To steal from a Gentile, the Talmud states, is worse than to steal from a Jew, because the sin of theft is compounded by the sin of profaning God's name. And the supreme act of sanctifying the name is to die for one's faith.

The examples presented in this and the previous section show us how the biblical writers approached religious ideas. They did not lack interest in speculative matters; but they were inclined rather to explore the varied possibilities that could be derived from an idea rather than to use it as a building block in a system.

● **Ezekiel the Theologian.** The attempt to arrive at a more organized structure was not, however, altogether absent; we can observe it in the prophet Ezekiel. We have had one instance of his doctrinaire reasoning. In what is perhaps the noblest passage in his book, God promises that He will give His people a new heart and spirit, and will replace their heart of stone with one of human flesh. But this moving assurance of divine grace is subordinated to the proposition that God must worry about His standing in the Gentile world.

Equally questionable was Ezekiel's doctrine of retribution. For a long time the Israelites believed in corporate responsibility: the entire community or nation might suffer for the misdeeds of a few, and vice versa. (This is in some measure an empirical fact.) But there was a growing recognition among biblical thinkers of the importance and value of the individual. Out of this consciousness of individual worth, Ezekiel formulated the doctrine that every person receives the exact reward or punishment he deserves, here in this life (Ezekiel 18). Disregarding all evidence to the contrary, he insisted that what he believed ought to happen is indeed what does happen.

The story of the Exodus contains another instance of the way that a doctrinaire position may have disturbing consequences. Doubtless, old tradition told of ten plagues that befell Egypt and led to the release of the Hebrew slaves. But when the story came to be written down, those who reflected on it were moved to ask: Why were so many plagues necessary? When misfortune followed misfortune on schedule, exactly as foretold, why did not Pharaoh let the people go? To provide some kind of answer, the writer resorted to a desperate theological expedient: God, he declared, hardened Pharaoh's heart, to provide more occasions for displaying His power! (Exodus 10:1, 2, etc.)

Perhaps it was such attempts at logical consistency—with results that were not only unconvincing, but morally shocking —that led Jewish thinkers to adopt a different way.

● **The Talmud.** We have seen examples of the "exploratory method" in the Bible. Before examining the second great classic of Judaism, the Talmud, some preliminary remarks are in order.

It would be a lengthy task to give an adequate description of that vast body of written material—the term "literature," in the ordinary sense of the word, does not apply to the Talmud. Let us simply note that its basic substance is law, or as its authors called it, *halakhah*—meaning roughly, "the way to go." This includes civil, criminal, and family laws, as well as religious duties and ritual procedures. It is based on the provisions of the Mosaic law, supplemented by much traditional material—and the whole is elaborated at great length and with endless detail.

This legal subject matter is presented in a sprawling, untidy form. But the lack of system applies only to arrangement and presentation. The substance is solid, the texture tightly woven. Legal issues are analyzed with keen and subtle logic. Conflicting views are vigorously debated to arrive at a final definition of the prevailing law. But where contradictions and discrepancies are not explicit ("Rabbi A says yes, Rabbi B says no"), an effort is usually made to harmonize conflicting statements. The disagreement is not real, the Talmud will say, because the seemingly contradictory utterances apply to slightly different situations.

Where the fact of dissent is not clearly indicated, continuity and consistency of viewpoint are generally assumed. The Rabbis will, on occasion, entertain the possibility that a scholar contradicted himself; or that he changed his mind on a point of law; or that in making a certain statement, he overlooked a tradition to the contrary; or that there were some variations of law and custom between Jerusalem and Galilee, and between Palestine and Babylonia. They also acknowledged certain differences of procedure as between civil, criminal, and ritual law. Nevertheless, they generally operated on the assumption that the entire *halakhah* is a single entity, and sometimes they resorted to forced reasoning to demonstrate this homogeneity and to iron out contradictions.

One sample will indicate how far they went in this assumption of unity.[7] A marriage is annulled because the bridegroom had not been informed in advance about some physical defect of the bride. What financial consequences follow? In attempting to elucidate the question, the Rabbis draw analogies from the laws of "leprosy" in Leviticus 13, from a case where two men "swap" animals, and from the ritual consequences of the discovery that the stomach of a slaughtered animal had been perforated by a swallowed needle.

But the Talmudic urge for logical consistency, even by the use of hairsplitting, applies only to legal discussions. In treating questions of theology, the Talmud displays an indifference to system that seems almost scandalous. "The Rabbis," said Solomon Schechter, "show a carelessness and sluggishness in the application of theological principles which must be most astonishing to certain minds, which seem to mistake merciless logic for God-given truth."[8] All nonlegal material was lumped together as *aggadah*—meaning roughly, "something told." Within this category are serious discussions of religious belief and moral obligation, edifying and often beautiful expositions of biblical texts and narratives, parables, tales about the deeds and sayings of the Rabbis themselves, and bits of popular wisdom and folklore, including an admixture of superstitions. In discussing *aggadah*, the Rabbis rarely employed the sharp critical methods they used in treating questions of law. They reasoned cogently and consistently about torts and bailments, about the validity of divorce documents, even about "that fatal egg which was laid on a festival," and which according to the prevailing view might not be eaten that day. But on basic questions of human destiny—the nature of God, revelation, the soul, sin and atonement, the future life of the individual, and the messianic age—they permitted wide latitude of speculation and expression. Divergent views were recorded side by side, with little or no attempt to harmonize them, or to choose between them. (Even when they went through the motions—"one statement refers to case A, the other to case B"—they were far less critical than when they dealt with *halakhah*.) Rarely did they attempt to define a belief which was binding on all the faithful. One who reads the compendia of Schechter and of George Foot Moore[9] will see how keen was the interest of the Rabbis in theological questions, and how profound many of their insights were—and yet how they refrained from the attempt to achieve creedal uniformity.

The situation is strange not only because of the contrast within the Talmudic sources between consistency in legal discussions and lack of system in theological matters, but also because of the contrast with the Hellenistic environment of the Rabbis. The impact of Greek language, customs, institutions, and ideas on Jewish life in the Talmudic period was enormous.[10] We know of direct contacts between the Rabbis on one hand, and pagan philosophers and Christian theologians on the other. Echoes of Hellenistic and Christian lore appear in many passages of rabbinic literature. The Jewish teachers knew about the intellectual enterprise of systematic philosophy and theology, and did not choose to engage in it.

● **Paradoxes of Rabbi Akiba.** Of this lack of theological system we offer a few extreme cases.

Philosophers were bedeviled for centuries by the problem of free will and providence. If God knows in advance what we are going to do, does this not deprive us of free choice? But if we are free to choose what we shall do, does this not imply that God doesn't yet know what our choice will be—thereby denying His omniscience? During the Middle Ages, a few Jewish thinkers accepted this contradiction as absolute, and felt themselves forced to make a choice. One opted for divine omniscience and determinism; another insisted on free will, admitting that God's knowledge is insofar limited. The majority of medieval Jewish philosophers tried to hold on to both human freedom and divine omniscience, and sought to harmonize them by various verbal devices.

But long before, a more radical position had been taken by Rabbi Akiba (he lived at the end of the first century C.E. and the beginning of the second). "All is foreseen," he asserted, "but free will is granted." The utterance is so brief that one might well be uncertain of its meaning were there not other rabbinical utterances to serve as commentary. One reads, "Everything is in the power of Heaven except the fear of Heaven." The second states that when conception takes place, God determines whether the person brought into being will be rich or poor, strong or weak, wise or foolish, but whether he will be righteous or wicked is not foreordained.

In short, Akiba denies any limit to God's knowledge, yet affirms man's moral responsibility in freedom. Logic, he implies, must bow to the needs of religious living.[11]

But he is not finished. He goes on to assert: "The world is judged with grace, yet all is according to the deeds performed."

The first part of his saying dealt with a perennial problem of philosophy; in the second he disposes of a continuing issue of theology. Does God reward and punish us according to our deserts, or does His redemptive grace deliver us from the consequences of our folly and sin? Akiba answers boldly, "Both!"

● **A Particle.** Another striking case deals with methodology in expounding Scripture. The Hebrew particle _eth_ often precedes a direct object, and is then untranslatable. In other constructions it means "with." Now there were those who believed that no word or letter of the Bible is superfluous; every detail must have meaning. From this standpoint, there must be a reason why _eth_ is sometimes inserted before the object and sometimes omitted. A certain Rabbi Nehemiah HaAmsoni therefore undertook to show that every _eth_ before a direct object has an inclusive force, comparable to "with"—that is, the verb applies not only to the explicit object, but to something else as well. He pursued this method throughout the Pentateuch until he came to Deuteronomy 10:20, "You must revere the Lord your God." Since _eth_ precedes the word for "the Lord," Nehemiah's norm required him to explain that we must revere someone else as we revere God. This he could not bring himself to do, and he terminated his enterprise abruptly. "What then," his pupils asked, "becomes of all your prior expositions?" He replied, "As I received a reward for expounding, so I receive a reward for stopping."[12] That is, he did not repudiate his norm, but refused to apply it in a situation where the results were religiously objectionable.

● **Return to the Present.** These examples illustrate sufficiently the unstructured theology taught by many Jewish teachers of the past. Their approach has greatly influenced the thinking contained in subsequent chapters of this book—but by way of suggestions rather than of rules. The Talmudic rabbis presented their teachings in sermonic form, attaching their insights to Bible verses which they explained imaginatively, often fantastically. We cannot mechanically adopt their way. It would not justify us in heaping up all sorts of notions in confusion, without attempt at classification or critical analysis. Even the Talmud, though it lacks a theological system, displays a certain unity of tone and some frequently recurring patterns of thought. And from the Middle Ages to the present, Jewish thinkers have made many attempts to construct an organized Jewish theology, in rationalistic, mystical, idealistic, or existentialist terms. Whether or not we accept any of these formulations as final, we cannot ignore them. Nor can we disregard the pervasive influence of the thought currents of our own scientific-minded age.

But in our own way we can, like the Talmudic sages, adopt an exploratory method, and retain a healthy skepticism about closed intellectual systems.

Chapter III ————————————————

KNOWLEDGE AND MORALS

T he Sources of Knowledge. Ancient thinkers recognized two sources of knowledge, sense and reason. The senses, they held, passively receive impressions from outside physical stimuli. Reason—inward, active, spiritual—operates on these data with independence and mastery. This account is now seen as much too simple. We now understand that sense perception requires attention—that to see we must look, and that what we see depends in part on what we are trained to see and what we expect to see. Nor are all sensory stimuli external; many come from within our own bodies.

Reason, on the other hand, is not the autonomous power it was once believed to be. It does not attain infallibility by following the canons of logic: we no longer recognize one simple all-sufficient system of logic. Our thinking is conditioned by our experience, in particular by our vocabulary, since we think chiefly in words. Moreover, our thought is colored and distorted by our emotions, including some drives of which we are not fully aware. The knowledge we garner from experience is a combination of the sensory and the rational; the two elements combine and influence each other.

There is, indeed, a physiological basis for distinguishing the two. Sensory experience is bound up with the various receptors of the nervous system; cerebration is associated with movements of the speech organs—even though we may not go as far as the behaviorists, who say that thought is nothing but the movements of the speech muscles.

It is a basic contention of this book that we have an additional source of knowledge in man's *moral sense*. This sense has no physiological counterpart. People ordinarily think of it as a mixture of rational and emotional elements. If this is so, the whole is here greater than the sum of its parts. Conversely, an analysis of the moral sense leaves a characteristic residue after the rational and emotional parts are abstracted.

Before we examine this contention further, it is proper to consider another question: Why should we not also regard the emotions as a source of knowledge? They do constitute a distinct group of psychological phenomena, associated as they are with visceral, vascular, and endocrine changes.

The answer is that in practice the emotions have little to teach us except their own existence. One who has never experienced fear, anger, or affection might find it hard to understand such reactions in others—like the boy in Grimm who wanted to learn to shudder. But otherwise the emotions instruct us hardly at all. Indeed, the more frequently and intensely we are gripped by an emotion, the less we are able to learn. But sense and reason (to say nothing of the moral sense we are about to examine) can yield a steady education if we are willing to accept it.

• **The Sense of "Ought."**   By the moral sense I mean man's capacity to respond to situations in terms of obligation, of "oughtness." This is not to say that we have innate ideas of right and wrong, or a conscience that infallibly directs us toward divinely appointed norms. But all the positivistic explanations of morality—psychological and sociological—appear to be insufficient.

All these views start from the premise that the individual is by nature amoral and selfish. Patterns of conduct are imposed on him by society because they are useful (or believed to be useful) for the perpetuation, stability, and comfort of the community. Family, tribe, school, and police impose these norms by giving praise and reward to those who obey and by punishing those who rebel. Eventually the rules become ingrained and internalized, so that the individual follows them even when no one is there to enforce them.

Such explanations, however plausible, are incomplete. For moral conduct is not always conformity to established rules. Sometimes our perception of ethical values compels us to dissent from the accepted patterns and to defy them, possibly with great danger, almost certainly with some discomfort. The prophets of Israel, who today are regarded as the great champions of righteousness, were denounced and persecuted in their own days as subversive and traitorous. If morality were no more than a response to the pressures of society, it would be hard to account for the rejection of accepted standards in the name of a higher morality.

A second consideration is that in some individuals the moral sense is feeble or even entirely absent. This may be the result of degrading conditions in which they grew up, but instances also emerge from families where good standards prevail; and plenty of decent people have survived the test of slum conditions. The amoral person is not necessarily unintelligent. He may have received a sound ethical training, and be able to discuss moral values in conventional terms. (I knew one such who was quite prudish on occasion.) But for his own conduct ethical values are not compelling or even relevant.

An instructive parallel to the moral sense is provided by the sense of humor. Different cultures have widely divergent notions of what is funny. But in all cultures, some individuals react vigorously to what is felt as comic, some feebly, others not at all. So it seems to be with the moral sense as well.

The relativity of moral standards is not an argument against the reality of the moral sense. Though prevailing standards of right and wrong are conditioned by the character and traditions of a particular society, their implementation requires a capacity to respond affirmatively to moral demands. That is what we mean by the moral sense, which may on occasion lead to a challenge to the accepted norms.

The relativity of morals can, incidentally, be overstated. Ruth Benedict's book _Patterns of Culture_ suggests a world without any fixed values. But when we turn from the relatively primitive societies she describes to more advanced civilizations, we find that the moral teaching of Greek, Indian, and Chinese sages, and that of the Jewish and Christian traditions, have much in common. One need not blink substantial disagreements over quietism and activism, authority and freedom, individuality and group solidarity, military glory and meek self-abnegation. But there are large areas of agreement regarding courage, responsibility, truthfulness, self-control, respect for rules, stability of the social order, and avoiding hurt to others. And though different societies have practiced many varied forms of marriage and have regulated relations between the sexes in different ways, virtually all societies have agreed that some control must be placed on sexual activity, and that in this connection a prime consideration is the welfare of children.

● **What Does the Moral Sense Teach?**   We have shown that most people have a moral sense; though composed of intellectual and emotional elements, it is more than a mixture of its components. We have argued further that it is not just a response to external pressures; for those in whom this sense is weak may evade the accepted standards of behavior, and those in whom this sense is exceptionally strong can transcend the conventional mores and attain to higher values.

But even if all this is true, how can the moral sense be a source of knowledge?

Let us approach an answer obliquely by noting that scientific knowledge cannot be attained without the exercise of moral qualities. The continuing drive to extend the frontiers of knowledge, the patience to carry out tiresome investigations in full awareness that they may prove futile, the willingness to accept unwelcome conclusions that demolish cherished theories, the self-discipline to avoid wrenching the data to fit a preconceived pattern or produce a desired result—all these are essentially character values. Intellectual integrity is at least as much a moral virtue as it is an intellectual virtue.

It may be objected that conscious distortion would subvert the entire scientific enterprise, but the question could still be asked: Why should men sacrifice interest or comfort to the scientific enterprise? The positivist can only reply that men have a stubborn curiosity, or that they find a quasi-aesthetic pleasure in scientific inquiry—but this reduces the undertaking to a matter of personal taste. If, however, one is weary or frustrated, why should he not abandon his monastic commitment to research for something more amusing and profitable? There have been numerous instances of scientific charlatanism for fame or cash, to say nothing of the manipulation of scientific materials to suit totalitarian political prejudices. And there is no *scientific* reason to condemn such aberrations.

There is a second way in which morality is related to knowledge. It is a specialized case of learning by doing, comparable to laboratory exercises, field trips, and other familiar educational procedures.

We start to learn politeness by being taught to say "Please" and "Thank you." At first this is a matter of conditioning children to give rote responses, but out of this mechanical reaction one may come to a comprehension of respect and consideration for others which are the essence of courtesy. In the same way, courage, unselfishness, and generosity acquire content and meaning for us only as we practice them. A virtue known only by observing it in others would be like a cricket game as seen by an American visitor to England. He knows that something meaningful is going on, but he doesn't quite grasp it, and wonders why people are so excited about it.

The same thing, indeed, may be said about the emotions. We have already noted that descriptions in books would never suffice to give us an understanding of fear, sorrow, or tenderness. But we also saw that the experience of such feelings teaches little beyond the nature of the emotion itself. Fear, for example, is just a feeling, but courage is a value. It can be assayed, analyzed, and applied. I doubt if moral values can be justified by logic; but they can be examined by reason, and their implementation can be governed by reason. By and large, values are heightened, clarified, and purified for us, when our intuitive grasp of them is supplemented by thoughtful study. But emotions can only be inspected clinically; when we try to examine our own feelings, they quickly evaporate.

Not all values, of course, are moral. Some are sensory, some esthetic, some economic. But many, perhaps most, value judgments contain a moral element, as well as rational and emotional components. This is certainly true of such explosive and controversial values as pride and power.

Now the area of values is the decisive area of human life. Existence is empty and frustrating for us if we do not have significant goals—and some standards to determine what is truly significant for us. It is chiefly man's moral nature, expressing itself, not in mere opinion but in action as well, which gives him access to this area of values.

Like the senses, like reason, our moral sense is limited and fallible. Just as the human eye can see only certain wave lengths (and even within those limits we sometimes make mistakes), just as our reasoning is sometimes fallacious—so it is with our moral powers. Our conscience is conditioned by environment and experience. It may be totally insensitive to a manifest wrong, simply because the latter is commonplace and familiar. Or it may overreact. And just as excessive light may cause blindness and excessive strain may disrupt our reasoning power, so too overwhelming pressure may destroy conscience. (That area has been explored with diabolic skill by the totalitarians. I suspect, however, that one who has been destroyed morally by torture or brainwashing feels a certain self-loathing that testifies to the former presence of a conscience, as an empty eye socket indicates that the person once could see.)

● **The Knowledge of God.** The moral sense, then, gives us important insights into life's meaning. We understand values truly when we choose them and live by them. I think, however, that we can go further and show how man's moral sense can lead him toward theological truth.

Much of the time moral conduct means conformity to the accepted rules of behavior in a given society. In these terms, it frequently pays to be good. Our rectitude evokes confidence and trust, our kindnesses are often reciprocated, our service to the community is lauded.

But there are times when righteousness is no longer profitable.

This happens when one feels called upon to go far beyond the ordinary requirements of duty—for example, to risk his own life in trying to save another. In such cases, the sacrifice may be easier because we are aware that it will be applauded and honored by the community—though we may still wonder about the value of praise for one who is no longer there to hear it. But even that solace is denied to one who for moral reasons takes a stand against a hostile majority, who gives up peace of mind, security, even life itself for the sake of a principle.

Such people do exist; such events do happen. One who is ready to part with life itself for the sake of a transcendent value testifies by his act to faith in an order of reality more important —more real—than the physical universe. (For ordinarily we think of life as the supreme value. What good are truth, goodness, love, if we are not present to experience them?) We cannot shrug off such instances because they are relatively rare —and perhaps they are not so rare as we suppose. Nor can we say that the individuals in question were driven like lemmings by an irresistible urge for self-destruction. The hero and martyr can be readily distinguished from the thrill-seeker and the suicide. These acts of self-abnegation, moreover, are not confined to those who believe in some sort of heaven where their momentary sacrifice will be rewarded by endless bliss.

Whatever their theology, or their lack of theology, those who are ready to endure suffering or death for a principle are affirming an order of existence more real and more compelling than the physical order revealed by our senses and made more coherent for us by science. They are, whether they know it or not, declaring their faith in the God of righteousness.

"Your father," said Jeremiah to a venal king, "dispensed justice and equity; he upheld the rights of the poor and needy. That is truly knowing Me—declares the Lord."[13] The supreme acts of morality affirm a cosmic righteousness. They are admittedly a demonstration of faith, not a scientific proof. (Though one may well ask how such acts are to be explained by the mechanics of Darwinism, and whether man's capacity to transcend himself does not point to a transcendent source of his moral strength.) But it is a most impressive demonstration. It confirms the power of the moral sense to give us insight into reality.

● **A Tentative Summing Up.** Let us bring together the contentions we have been examining. Our theology must take into account the data of experience, the discourse of reason, and the insights of man's moral nature. We must not, however, expect that the data we derive from these sources of knowledge can all be incorporated into a single integrated and inwardly consistent whole. Even in the natural sciences, with their more limited and sharply defined subject matter, their precise measurements and austere method, an overall synthesis has not been possible; many loose ends and discrepancies baffle researchers. For theologians, concerned as they are with intangibles, a seamlessly unified view of life, including those intangibles as well as the materials of science, seems altogether beyond reach.

The history of philosophy is strewn with the ruins of systems, as Agrigento and Baalbek are strewn with the ruins of temples, magnificent but uninhabitable. The classical philosophers apparently supposed that all the essential data were known to them, insofar as things are knowable at all. The task of philosophy was to arrange the known data in a symmetrical and meaningful pattern. Even Aristotle, who eagerly collected information about "natural history," hardly entertained the notion that new discoveries might require a modification of his views about the universe and about human behavior.

The scholastics of the Middle Ages made such assumptions explicit: the Bible and Aristotle provide all the data we need. The information is available, the main outlines of the synthesis of revelation and reason are fairly clear. All that remains is to elaborate details and make sure they are consistent with the whole.

But today everyone is aware that our knowledge is growing at an explosive rate. The advance is not only the expansion of raw data—say, the discovery of hitherto unknown species of ferns —or of practical applications—say, the production of new rocket fuels. Today we are often called upon to adjust our minds to revolutionary concepts, as in mathematical physics and genetics.

Man cannot help trying to organize the information he acquires, to see the bits and chunks of fact in some kind of ordered pattern. But manifestly any summary of scientific information is tentative and subject to revision. It is orderly and reasonable, as the arrangement of books in a library is orderly and reasonable. But such an arrangement does not necessarily correspond to the order of the universe or even to the structure of human thought. It is determined in considerable measure by the number, sizes, and subjects of the books presently in the collection. Next year it may be necessary to reclassify and reshelve many volumes that are here now, as the result of new accessions.

Or we may say that any contemporary scientific synthesis is a trial balance, not a final audit. Any attempt to round it out by inference and extrapolation is chancy. We may learn tomorrow that symmetries we had assumed do not in fact exist, and that an area we thought we understood is far more complex than we supposed. Einstein's repeated and unsuccessful efforts to devise a unified field theory should be a sobering reminder.

But the attempt to organize all experience into a structure that suits our human intelligence is more than an error of method. It is also a manifestation of *chutzpah*. The systematic theologian does more than disregard the tentative nature of our scientific conclusions: he also ignores a basic religious truth. For theology deals with a reality we may be able to touch, but cannot enfold and encircle. If we could define God—that is, draw a line around Him—what our line enclosed would not be God. Even the fundamentalist must recognize that the Bible—and the same would apply to any other sacred document—does not provide us with enough information to construct a model of the cosmos; it proposes no more than to offer human beings guidance for life in the presence of God.

• **Some Warnings.**   If the worst effect of too much theological or philosophic consistency were to involve us in intellectual tangles, we could afford to be tolerant about it. Even here, indeed, the issue of intellectual integrity will not down. A jigsaw puzzle is not solved properly until every piece falls into place, without forcing. But it has always been characteristic of system-builders that they ended up with some pieces missing and others left over. They tried to squeeze in the odd parts, but they never really fitted; that is why the old system was always discarded or drastically modified and a new one attempted. But much greater evils, tragic evils, have resulted from excess of logic.

For the most savage cruelty has often been inflicted in the name of high principles and sublime ideals. Relentless per-secution has been justified—one might say necessitated—by carrying dogmas to their logical conclusion. It makes sense to torture and burn heretics to save their souls from damna-tion and to protect others from a similar fate—that is, it makes sense if one argues consistently from the assumption that there is one true Church, acceptance of whose teachings alone can provide escape from eternal torment. Similarly, the liquidation of the kulaks, the Siberian prison camps, thought control, and other horrors of our age are reasonable inferences from the dogma that communism is the paradise destined inevitably for humanity by the inscrutable forces of economic determinism (in theological terms, the will of God).

The horrors we have alluded to are not to be regarded as mere outbursts of savagery and their theoretical justification as no more than rationalization. Behind any action or policy there is, of course, a tangle of motives. Lust for power and sadism are realities, and we need not deny the brutal instincts manifest in any act of brutality. But religious or political doctrine has often imparted a special savagery to such acts. Those who performed them have felt a sense of rectitude, even of sanctity, in doing things they would otherwise have shrunk from.

This is especially plain when the victim of logical consistency is one who assents to it. The victims of Calvinism included not only Servetus and those killed by the Scotchish covenanters, but many Calvinists as well. Of Jonathan Edwards, the great Calvinist preacher, Ernest Sutherland Bates has written: "This imposing system of thought [i.e., Calvinism as Edwards un-derstood it], which did violence to every natural instinct of human kindness, was not reached by Edwards without personal agony. His was naturally a peculiarly delicate and sensitive temperament, delighting in physical beauty and quickly responsive to beauty of character. His intense mystical faith in the reality of perfection made every instance of human depravity something utterly shocking and unforgivable. He was filled with love toward man, nature, and God; but constrained by his logic to sacrifice the lesser to the greater, he did not hesitate; nevertheless his personality was wrenched and distorted in the process."[14]

No such conflicts seem to have troubled Michael Wigglesworth, author of a "poem" on the last judgment. (He died in 1705, when Edwards was two years old.) In it he deals with the plight of those who died in infancy, tainted with original sin, and not predestined for salvation. They protest before the heavenly tribunal that they are innocent, but God replies:

> *You sinners are; and such a share*
> *   As sinners may expect,*
> *Such you shall have, for I do save*
> *   None but Mine own elect.*
> *Yet to compare your sins with theirs*
> *   Who lived a longer time,*
> *I do confess yours is much less,*
> *   Though every sin's a crime.*
> *A crime it is, therefore in bliss*
> *   You may not hope to dwell;*
> *But unto you I shall allow*
> *   The easiest room in hell.*[15]

Here consistency is vindicated at the price of making God a capricious (not to say, silly) tyrant, whose behavior any decent human being would be ashamed to emulate.

A friend of mine once commented at this point that reasoning is never better than the assumptions with which it starts, and that my examples do not prove the danger of logical consistency. Torquemada and Stalin, Wigglesworth and Edwards argued from false premises, and it was these—not consistency

—that led to their dreadful conclusions. There is a double answer to this. First, it is precisely when the logical consequences of a premise are morally repugnant that we should feel the obligation to reexamine the premise. Second, the most valid premise may lead to trouble if it is pushed too far.

● **Some Acknowledgments.** Here it is proper to pause and make acknowledgment of the sources on which I have drawn thus far. My chief debt is to the Rabbis of the Talmud, for many individual insights, and especially for the striking contrast between their lack of system in theology and their definiteness and precision in the treatment of law.

I have often felt a sort of identity between the Talmudic approach to theology and the pragmatism of William James. In both cases there is willingness to explore the possibilities of a variety of ideas, and to consider their practical effects on life and conduct. The analogy should not be pressed too far. The Rabbis all assumed that Scripture was absolute and inerrant truth— even though in fact they derived multiple meanings from it.

Perhaps even more relevant is the principle of polarity so much stressed by Morris Raphael Cohen. According to this principle, opposites may be true at one and the same time. Truth is not a middle ground between extremes, as Aristotle suggested, nor is it approached by the synthesis of opposing forces, as Hegel taught. It is rather the uneasy balance and tension between opposites.[16]

The contention that man's moral nature is a possible source of knowledge no doubt has some connection with the teaching of Kant, but the differences are worth stressing. I have not been dealing with ethical absolutes or categorical imperatives. Nor do I assert that certain extensive theological affirmations are the necessary postulates of man's moral nature. I suggest no more than that man's capacity for moral response gives him certain insights into reality that sense and reason alone cannot provide. And there is no denying that our moral instincts, like our sensory powers and our reason, are limited and fallible. We must make do with what we have.

Further, I cannot accept Kant's insistence that there is no good but a good will. The repudiation of "eudaemonism"—the notion that goodness may or should lead to happiness—by Kant's faithful follower Hermann Cohen seems to me overdone and needlessly indignant. An ethical decision or action must be judged not only by the purity of its motives, but also by its practical consequences. More harm has been done by some well-meaning men of virtue who did not foresee the effects of their choices than by many a cynical scoundrel who at least knew what he was doing. There is perhaps no Talmudic saying more characteristic than the injunction to "be clever in the fear of God."[17]

GOD AND EVIL:
THE PROBLEM OF OUR AGE

T he crucial theological issue of our time is the problem of evil. The words "of our time" must be stressed. The problem is indeed perennial; it occurs not only in the abstract speculations of professors, but in the pained outcry "Why should this misfortune have happened to a nice guy like me?" The question was asked in ancient Sumer and Babylon, in a world inhabited by a multitude of unstable and easily offended gods and by swarms of evil spirits and demons. In such a world, the existence of evil was not a theoretical problem; it was clearly the work of hostile demons or angry deities. And yet men still asked "Why?" With the appearance of monotheism, the issue became far more acute and agonizing. How can a single righteous God tolerate so much evil?

And yet suffering has not always been the central problem of religious thinkers. The age of Maimonides was far more troubled about the issue of philosophy versus revelation. Maimonides does indeed touch on the problem of evil, but his chapters on the subject are not among the more profound sections of his *Guide of the Perplexed*. No doubt the scholastics were less concerned about present evil because they believed that the imbalance would be corrected after death and in the messianic age.

Similarly, the nineteenth-century theologians were busy

grappling with the challenges of Darwinism and the critical approach to the Bible; the problem of evil was not their chief worry. In facing the latter, they were sustained by the predominant faith in progress; they were confident that scientific technology and the spread of popular education would soon eliminate most of the errors and ills that still plagued mankind.

It is no doubt the crushing disappointment at the results of our progress that accounts in great measure for the mood of resentment and despair that pervades our world today. We hoped for so much, but nothing has turned out the way we expected. Even medical research—which all of us regard as desirable—has not proved an unmixed blessing. Infant mortality has been sharply reduced, infectious diseases have been brought under control—and now we have the horrors of the population explosion and the likelihood of mass starvation on an unparalleled scale. We have likewise prolonged the life of the aged—not only for the tranquil and loved, but also for the lonely and decrepit and, still worse, for the hopelessly senile.

Such things have happened when scientific knowledge was applied with the highest of motives. But too often the new skills have been exploited for shamelessly evil purposes. We have lived through two world wars and innumerable smaller ones. We have experienced the rise of new and uniquely efficient forms of tyranny which employ modern weaponry to suppress dissent, and new forms of mass communication to impose mindless conformity. The cruelest savagery ever recorded arose in a nation known for its high rate of literacy, its scientific achievements, and its devotion to culture. No wonder we are bitterly disillusioned.

We have also learned to our dismay that even those segments of society that possess material comfort and educational advantage are subject to restlessness, ennui, and rebelliousness. Alcoholism, drug addiction, family breakdown, and even violence exist in suburbs as well as slums.

And so we hear many voices proclaiming that existence is utterly absurd and therefore evil. Secular existentialism seems an utterly bleak philosophy, and the Christian existentialists do not say very much that is different: they simply end their doleful account of things with an unexpected "Hallelujah."

The mood of the age is cosmically negative: existence is meaningless, God is dead. Yet the evils that evoked this reaction were basically man-made. Our world is not darkened so much by a Lisbon earthquake or by the persistence of malignant disease as by the effects of human shortsightedness, greed, and cruelty. Those Jewish thinkers who reject God or rage against Him are haunted by the memory of the Holocaust.

• **A Word about Auschwitz.** There are no words, no concepts adequate to the facts of the Holocaust. It was not a spontaneous outbreak of popular blood lust, but a coldly conceived program of extermination, carried out with highly organized efficiency. To facilitate the physical destruction of the victims, their moral degradation and corruption were also deliberately planned. The ghastly deeds of the Nazis are beyond description and beyond comprehension. And these crimes were compounded by the failure of the "democratic" nations to do anything to stop the slaughter long after they well knew what was happening in the death camps.

But it is not clear why so many theologians should regard Auschwitz as a boundary mark in the history of religious thought. What Auschwitz teaches, if it teaches anything, is that we have underestimated man's capacity for evil. We have too often assumed that men are guided by self-interest, and that their evil deeds are the result of a misguided urge to protect or aggrandize themselves. We have not recognized that men may be attracted to evil because it is evil, may even embrace it in a mad ecstasy. But our failure to take this fact into account does not mean that it never had been known. An attentive reading of the Bible makes plain the truth that moral evil is sometimes more than mere deficiency; it can be a dynamic, demonic force in human life.

Yet one may doubt that Auschwitz revealed any new truth about God or His relation to man. We can understand that a group of Jews, forced to watch the death agony of a child hanged in retaliation for an act of resistance, should have cried out "Where is God?" In such a moment no one can be a philosopher. But the proper question was still "Where is man?"

But why should God have made man so bad, even so potentially bad?

Here we come back to the old, old question of human freedom.

● **The Choice.** If we believe that human freedom exists at all —in whatever measure—and that man is capable of moral choices, we believe that man has the capacity to do wrong as well as right. But we ordinarily underestimate man's possibilities at both ends of the moral scale. The "golden mean" may or may not be an adequate ethical principle but, in fact, most of us would like to lead our lives a little on the good side of mediocrity, without being under too much moral strain.

> The number of people who want to be a hero
> Is practically zero.

But experience teaches us that men do rise to heights of heroism and saintliness, as they also sink to levels of unspeakable villainy.

Of course, the reality of human freedom has been repeatedly denied. Man has been depicted by pagans as the puppet of fate, by Muslims and Calvinists as predestined by God to run a certain course, by mechanistic philosophers and scientists as the product of all previous causation, by Marx as controlled by economic forces, by Freud as irresistibly moved by inner forces of which he is not aware. No one can reasonably assert man's absolute independence. Henley's "I am the master of my fate, I am the captain of my soul" is much too inflated. But the intuition (or if you will, the postulate) that man has at least a measure of choice in his own actions is something I believe we are justified in clinging to.

Not that one can settle the debate by logical argument. But so powerful is this intuition that those who deny its validity and insist that it is a mere illusion still act as if they had freedom of choice. Sit a determinist (of any stripe—theological, scientific, Marxian, Freudian) at a lunch table with a voluntarist, and give each a bill of fare. You will not be able to determine from their words and their behavior which is which.

Moreover, all the positivistic arguments for determinism are tangled in a curious paradox. If our ideas and actions are governed by forces within the unconscious, the same applies to the theories of Freud. If they are determined by the sum total of our previous conditioning, the same applies to the doctrines of behaviorism. If they are under the iron rule of economic forces, the same applies to the teachings of Marx. If any one of these theories is valid, the discoverer of that theory must have been subject to the same inescapable powers that govern all human behavior. There is no way in which he could have broken out into a world of abstract "truth."

Further, it is precisely Sartre, that thoroughgoing pessimist, who stresses the centrality of personal decision. If man can choose between good and evil, then the evil that men do cannot be blamed on the cosmos. Auschwitz may be the terrible price that has been paid for human freedom.

• **The Twofold Reality.** But to return to the central problem, our method requires us to take full account of two realities: the existence of evil and the existence of good.

There have been many ingenious attempts to reduce evil to something else: it is unreality and illusion, it is the mere absence of good, it is blessing in disguise, it is an indispensable ingredient in "the best of all possible worlds." None of these verbal tricks will do. A little more impressive is the logical argument that good can be known only in distinction to bad, as the concept of "up" has meaning only in contrast to the concept of "down." But we could still ask: Why is there so much bad, and why is it so very bad? We could have learned the distinction quite well on the basis of a smaller helping. Physical pain is no doubt a biological necessity: a person who is completely analgesic is in constant danger. But why must so many persons endure intense agony for a long time, and to no avail? Insanity and idiocy, congenital deformity, painful and devastating disease, natural disasters, and on the other hand, moral evil that can be diabolic —such things are not to be lightly brushed aside or explained away.

The hope that some of these evils can be overcome—even the

fact that some have already yielded to scientific attack—is small comfort to those who came too soon to profit by new advances. We have, moreover, seen that the solution of one problem may create another problem. Above all, we are disquieted because moral progress has not kept pace with scientific and technological advance. Indeed there are those, not necessarily obscurantists, who wonder whether the kind of thinking that leads to scientific achievement may not have some connection with the increasing ruthlessness of what we call modern civilization.

Death has not been included among the evils enumerated above. In Christian thought, indeed, sin and death are regarded as inseparable, and redemption from sin brings with it redemption from death. In Judaism there is a variety of opinions. One third-century rabbi did assert that there is no death without prior sin, but there were others who rejected this view. An earlier teacher made a note in his copy of Genesis, opposite the words "God saw all that He had made and found it very good." "Very good," he wrote, refers to death.[16] Death remains uncanny and utterly ambiguous. No one who has seen terminal cancer or senile decay can regard it as the worst of evils. Perhaps death in itself (as distinguished from untimely and painful death) is not evil at all.

If the Stoics, Leibnizians, and Christian Scientists minimized evil too easily, or even denied it altogether, many moderns have gone to the opposite extreme. They dwell on everything ugly and painful, and shrug off beauty and goodness. It is sheer prejudice to denounce or sneer at those who view the world through rose-tinted glasses, and then to glorify the realism of those who see existence as unrelieved darkness. If, despite Mary Baker Eddy, sickness and pain are real, are health and joy any less real? They too exist.

There is beauty in the world of nature, there are delights of the senses* and the mind. There are still happy families—husbands

---

*Apropos the delights of the senses, I call attention to a peculiar phenomenon of contemporary literature: it is steeped in sexuality and still takes potshots at Puritan morals, but much present-day fiction

and wives who understand and sustain each other, parents who are neither neglectful nor overpossessive, and children who respect and love their parents, even though they don't always follow their advice. Above all, moral goodness is a reality, even though it is not, and never has been, in oversupply.

From the Darwinian standpoint, man's viciousness and cunning are readily explicable as advantages in the struggle to survive; his capacity for self-sacrifice, his devotion to unseen values are not so easy to explain. Tribal loyalties could indeed be accounted for: there is a drive to preserve the species as well as the individual. But how do we explain in Darwinian terms the lonely idealist, the devotee of truth or beauty, the one who follows his own vision, regardless of the cost?

We do not ordinarily agonize over the mystery of goodness. We take it for granted that it is right and proper for us to have pleasant experiences. It is only when we encounter frustration and suffering that we ask questions, often in anger. But in fact the goodness and wonder of life are as great a mystery as the evil and pain. In a baccalaureate sermon, President Conant of Harvard once pondered this double mystery and concluded that we are justified in affirming "a cautious but optimistic theism."[19] Less restrained is A. J. Heschel's rhapsody on man's sense of wonder, his talent for "radical amazement."[20] The fact of goodness, beauty, and wonder in human existence is just as solid and stubborn a fact as the presence of evil, ugliness, sorrow, and boredom. The twofold problem is there; it does not lend itself to any easy solution.

• **Nickles's Ditty.** In _J.B.,_ Archibald MacLeish's modernization of the Job drama, the poet puts this ditty into the mouth of Nickles, his version of Satan:

> _If God is God, He is not good;_
> _If God is good, He is not God._

The expression is neat; the argument is not new. The extent and

---

presents sexual activity as anything but joyous. Rather it appears as a painful, unrewarding obsession. Perhaps our age is not as liberated as it thinks.

severity of what we regard as undeserved suffering forces us to one of two conclusions—either God is indifferent to human need, if He exists at all; or He is not all-powerful and so shares in the suffering He cannot prevent. There is some precedent in Jewish thought for the second alternative, the idea of a limited, perhaps an emerging God,[21] though the meaning of such a term as "finite God" is not easy to grasp. Without ruling out this alternative here, I am constrained to challenge the dogmatism of Nickles. For dogmatism can be negative as well as positive.

Satan, according to old tradition, is an impudent fellow; because we have long known that, we should not let ourselves be taken in by him. We must ask: Does our human logic apply to cosmic matters? Must not the attempt to apply the categories of our earthbound thought to a divine order prove self-contradicting and self-defeating? If our human mind could encompass divinity, what it encompassed would not be divinity!

We shall see later on that the dilemma stated so deftly in *J.B.* was not accepted by the author of the biblical book of Job. But here, in contrast to the easy assurance of Nickles, let us ponder the words of Claude G. Montefiore: "I can have faith that the good and wise God has his own adequate solution of evil and suffering; but that a godless world produced goodness and knowledge, reason and love—this I cannot believe at all."[22] This is not only humbler than the chant of MacLeish, it is also more realistic. For without blinking or minimizing the evil, it takes sufficient note of the good as well.

• **One Step Forward.** So we are left with a contradiction we cannot resolve, the tension remains. But we can go a little further before we leave the subject. We have the possibility of controlling and correcting both physical and moral evil. It is true that our powers are not unlimited and absolute, and even our well-meaning efforts sometimes turn out badly. Like physical medicines, our moral medicines sometimes produce unfortunate side effects. But when physicians encounter such a problem, they do not give up the practice of their profession, nor do they go back to prescribing jalap and applying leeches. They try to develop a drug which will be as effective as the one they discarded, without the damaging side effects. This is what we must do as we strive to cure the ills of society. For it is the continuing struggle against evil and want that gives our life meaning.

It is becoming more and more evident that lack of work is as destructive as lack of food. This is evident today in the appalling phenomenon of youth gangs, whose destructive and criminal behavior results not from desperation born of hunger, but from lack of purpose and of meaningful activity in a society which has little use for their labor. Even if the automated welfare state of the future could provide for the material needs of everyone, it would still be a hell for masses of people who had no choice but to live indefinitely at public expense without contributing to the public good. Most people cannot accept the notion that they are useless and have no share in the world's work; and those who do accept it are a burden to themselves and a potential danger to society. It is a dreadful thing to be crushed by anxiety, but a life in which we never have anything to worry about may be even harder to endure. Too much security is as damaging as too little.

Ultimately, the world we know is the only kind of world in which the moral act is possible. If virtue were always rewarded and vice always punished, no one could be moral or immoral; he could only be prudent or imprudent. The wrongdoer would be like one who deliberately eats something he knows will make him acutely sick. If virtue were always crushed and vice always triumphant, morality would be barely possible—for potential martyrs. But in our world we see no clear relation between our deserts and our fortunes. Some good people are lucky, and some reprobates come to grief; but the reverse is equally true. It is only in such a situation that we can make a true moral decision, choosing to do the right because it is right, with the hope—but no assurance—that it will turn out well. And it is the possibility of making such a choice that gives our existence meaning and dignity.

● **The Biblical Job.** The considerations just mentioned are certainly helpful; yet they are just a mitigation, not a solution, of the problem with which we began. They are, moreover, directly relevant to the understanding of the Book of Job (in contrast with MacLeish's paraphrase), a work which is surely among the most profound and powerful achievements of the human spirit.

Those who regard the book as fundamentally skeptical seem to have misread it completely. It does not conclude that God does not exist, or that He is indifferent or hostile to man. Unorthodox as it is, it affirms a positive religious faith. This is the essence of the tragedy. Job will not submit to the judgment of his friends that his suffering is a deserved punishment. But he cannot accept the (seemingly logical) conclusion that God does not care. He pleads with God, rages at Him, challenges Him, but he does not turn away from Him. At the end he is told that he cannot expect to understand God's purposes and His ways, and Job accepts this as a response from God, a revelation of God's presence. His final word is not one of despair, but of reverent humility. Yet when God revealed Himself, He condemned the traditional theologians who distorted the truth in their zeal to defend Him; and He vindicated Job, who stormed at Him in protest. The riddle remains unsolved, but the faith in God's goodness endures.

Chapter V ═══════════════════════════════

WHAT CAN WE SAY
ABOUT GOD?

T he Ultimate Question of Belief. The preceding section is
an attempt to show that the realities of evil and suffering,
though they make faith in a good God difficult, do not
make it impossible. But it is necessary to bring into somewhat
clearer focus the meaning we attach to the phrase "a good God."

We should first notice that religious discourse cannot be
distinguished from nonreligious discourse by the presence or
absence of the vocable "God." Buddhism is frequently
mentioned as an instance of a religion which has no concept of
God, at least not in the Western sense. And it certainly is
possible to speak of God and to affirm His (or Its) existence
without any sense of religious feeling or commitment. People
use the same word in a great variety of ways.

The religious affirmation is rather that the universe is in some
way concerned with, and supportive of, man's needs and
aspirations.

One may express his faith in childlike terms: "God loves me."
Or one may follow Mordecai M. Kaplan in speaking of those
factors in the world that make for "salvation"[23] — i.e., human
fulfillment—and apply the name God to the sum total of those
factors. Whatever the deficiencies of such a God-concept, it
certainly implies that a measure of salvation is attainable—that
is, that the universe is so ordered that man may achieve a

meaningful existence in it. And this must mean something more
than the fact that human beings, having evolved on this planet,
can survive on it for the present. For that is an empirical
observation, not a religious affirmation. Kaplan certainly means
also that the universe provides conditions favorable to the
development and maintenance of spiritual values: such indeed,
is the plus which converts mere survival into salvation. Whether
in its naive or in its sophisticated version, the faith is still
essentially the same: that man is not a stranger in an
environment totally hostile or indifferent to him.

Here again we find ourselves confronting two kinds of
evidence that seem mutually contradictory. On the one hand,
the unimpassioned observation of human life and the scientific
study of natural phenomena seem to indicate that "nature" is
oblivious of, and indifferent to, the fate of the individual and the
fate of the species. All living creatures die sooner or later, mostly
sooner; and innumerable species have vanished through the
millennia. The same fate may overtake our species as well; and it
appears that entropy could bring about the end of all life on this
planet, if men don't destroy it sooner. A majestic cosmic power
is a reasonable inference (not a proved certainty) from the ordered complexity of our world. But it is not easy to discover the
God of Love in the struggle for existence.

Yet we cannot overlook the existence of those values which
are cherished by human beings—truth, beauty, goodness, love
—and to which the universe is said to be indifferent. Strangely,
those thinkers who consider themselves naturalists assume a total
discontinuity between man's hopes and dreams and the rest of
the universe. Yet from their scientific standpoint they must
regard man as a part of nature: His body is composed of the
same materials, and functions by the same physical and
chemical mechanisms, found in other creatures. True, in his case
evolutionary processes have led to an unprecedented complexity
of structure and still more of function, but the difference is
regarded by scientists as one of degree rather than of kind. It has
been assumed that there is some kind of continuity from
inorganic crystalline substances through the viruses to primitive

biological organisms and so on up the evolutionary ladder. Now if man is physiologically a native, how can he be spiritually an alien?

It has already been suggested that a purely mechanistic concept of evolution is inadequate to explain the emergence of human traits that do not make for self-preservation. The unselfish, compassionate saint, the truth-seeker, the poet and visionary are not well equipped for survival. On the other hand, we are not arguing for the kind of evolutionary system proposed by such thinkers as Lecomte de Nouilly and Teilhard de Chardin. We are simply contending that the values cherished and exemplified by some men sometimes _must_ have originated _within_ the universe. (This is especially compelling for those naturalistic thinkers who reject out of hand any notion of a divine revelation.) And if the origin of these values is natural, there can be no further talk about man as an utter stranger in this world. The matrix of his physical being is also the matrix of his loftiest visions and noblest aspirations.

Thus, despite the evidence to the contrary, we have a right to say that the universe is somehow concerned with man's needs and dreams, and thereby offers him some hope of fulfillment. Or, put in traditional terms, God cares about man and man's actions. Both the source of our hope and the source of our despair are dark and mysterious. A clear-cut solution of the riddle seems beyond attainment, but the decision of faith is at least as defensible as that of denial.

● **The Agnostic's Dilemma.** One studies a problem of pure science, of history, of philosophy, and finds insufficient evidence to support any hypothesis; or he finds contradictions which he is unable to resolve. In such a case he is fully justified in leaving the matter open until he turns up new or better evidence, or until he finds a legitimate way of reconciling the contradictory data. Indeed, he is obliged to do so, after he has gone as far as he can in his present researches.

This luxury of suspended judgment is not permitted a physician who must decide on the treatment of a critically sick patient. Shall he advise an operation, or some other risky procedure? He may be able to postpone a decision for a time, but to all intents and purposes, a long-delayed decision is a negative decision.

The same situation applies in the case of moral choices, where one has conflicting obligations, or where it is not easy to conclude what course of action will be best for those affected by the decision. However painful the problem may be, we have only so much time to make up our minds, otherwise our minds will be made up for us by others, or by the course of circumstances— and not always in the best way.

The agnostic who isn't sure whether he should believe in God or not is in a similar position. For what is at stake is not merely a question of philosophic probability. The matter involves a commitment of the whole personality. If the agnostic leads a godly life, he is thereby affirming God, whatever terminology he may employ and whatever theoretical reservations he may make.[24] If not, he might as well call himself an atheist and be done with it. For by acting as if there were no God, or as if the question were not of major importance, he has already made his choice.

• **Anthropomorphism.**   One of the Greek philosophers noted that the gods of the Germans are described as blue-eyed, and those of the Africans as flat-nosed; he added that if horses had gods, they would depict them as horses. The Bible protests not only against the representation of God by images, but also against our ascription to Him of human weaknesses and frailties (see, e.g., Isaiah 40:14 ff., 55:8 ff.; Psalm 50:21). Yet in many places the Bible itself seems to picture God as having both the appearance and the feelings of a human being.

When Aramaic translations of the Bible were prepared for popular use, they paraphrased such passages, to avoid giving the impression that God has a body like ours, or that He is subject to our limitations and weaknesses. Talmudic literature often explains such anthropomorphic expressions as a concession to our feeble power of understanding.

Medieval Jewish thinkers, schooled in Graeco-Arabic philosophy, were still more systematic and thorough in their efforts to correct the errors of literalism, and to eliminate all anthropomorphism from the concept of Diety. This was a passionate concern of Maimonides. Yet it seems that this great thinker ended up with a vision of God in the likeness of a tranquil Aristotelian philosopher. It is virtually impossible for us to escape a measure of anthropomorphism. We can't get outside our own skins, and we need not be unhappy that we are compelled to think in human terms. We can free ourselves from the grosser errors. We no longer believe that God enjoys the smell of burning fat, or even that he worries about His reputation among the Gentiles.[25] But I doubt if we can conceive of a God worth worshiping who is not to some extent formed in our image.

If a fish attempted to form a concept of Man, he would be able to think of this being only as an extraordinarily powerful fish. His concept of Man would be incomplete and in many respects downright mistaken: men do not have fins and gills. Nevertheless this ichthyomorphic concept would be closer to the truth than the view of some fishy intellectuals that man is a self-propelling fishnet, or of some others that "Man" is a mere figure of speech for the wetness of water.

And so we need not apologize for the statement that to believe in God in religious terms is to affirm that the universe is in some way concerned with, and supportive of, our human needs and longings. Obviously, God is very different from man; this is a basic teaching of Judaism, which has always insisted that God never becomes man and man never becomes God. When we ascribe intelligence, will, and goodness to God, we must never forget that we ordinarily apply such terms to physical beings of the genus *Homo,* living together in a society. Applied to God, they must have a very different (but perhaps not absolutely different) set of meanings. Yet a God lacking these qualities of personality (there is no other term we can use) would be inferior to us. Should the universe crush a man, remarked Pascal, the man would still be superior to what kills him, because he knows that he dies and is aware of the advantage which the universe has over him. The universe knows nothing about it. For "universe," substitute "impersonal god."

• **"Cash Value."**   According to William James, the meaning of a philosophic assertion is no more or less than the practical implications of the assertion for human life, its consequences for action, and the emotional attitudes which it sustains or negates. This is what James meant when he spoke in his colorful way of the "cash value" of an idea, a phrase which only the humorless could misinterpret. It seems to me that there is a certain kinship here with the ways of rabbinic thought.

For the Talmud frequently asks concerning a statement, "What consequences follow from it?" It is the ethical or ritual implications of a theological idea which interest the Rabbis. For example, they tolerate and quote a great variety of opinions about the nature of angels, but they are unanimous and emphatic in forbidding prayer to angels.

Now whether in fact the content of a philosophic idea is exhausted by the examination of its practical consequences can be argued, but it seems clear that James's method is a useful and fruitful one. It is disturbing to recall the bitter debates among the early Christian theologians over tenuous abstractions that seem utterly remote from human concerns. Why should they have fought so violently over issues that had no consequences either for personal piety or communal action?[26] One might argue that in speaking of things divine, men should state the truth as precisely as possible, but this hardly explains or justifies the hostility generated in these controversies.

The contrast with Judaism is striking. The few controversies within the Jewish community that resulted in charges of heresy and the formation of sects concerned issues that had far-reaching consequences in law, observance, and the forms of community life.

And our own assertion that theological propositions must be subjected not only to rational scrutiny, but also to moral evaluation, is not far from the pragmatic position.

● **The Cash Value of Pantheism.**   In view of the present popularity of various oriental and pseudo-oriental religions, it may be profitable to examine briefly the pragmatic difference between pantheism and monotheism.

No doubt the term pantheism covers a variety of

phenomena.* In India it appears to be primarily a kind of cosmic mysticism. For Spinoza, it was rather an intellectual intuition that all phenomena, sensory or mental, constitute a single causal system, outside which nothing exists.

In any form, pantheism appears to be a viewpoint that relieves tension. If God is all and all is God, I too share in the godhead; there is no creature, however primitive, and no human being, however debased, who is not here and now a part of God. Pantheism does not assert that the individual has divine traits or divine possibilities, but that he shares in divinity just as he is. There is then no transcendent moral demand. If the terms "God" and "Nature" are interchangeable (as Spinoza held), any kind of conduct, being natural, can also be regarded as divine.

It has been rightly pointed out that the word "unnatural" has been improperly used by moralists. It is sheer dogmatism to describe incest or buggery as "unnatural." Whatever exists in nature is _ipso facto_ natural. This applies not only to sexual deviations, about which we have grown more tolerant, but also to cruelty and murder, which most of us still condemn.

The pantheist has no mandate to change himself, still less the world. His perception of the pantheist "truth" should lead him to merge himself, a fragment of divinity, into the totality of God. The method may be the discipline that leads to the blissful goal of Nirvana or the more sober practice of the intellectual love of God.

Monotheism, however, is in the nature of a confrontation. Man is not God, even though he has the potential to become godly. There is an enescapable tension when he faces the divine. He must reckon with a will not his own, which he must either obey or resist. The monotheist has a task, whether it be expressed in the poetry of the prophetic challenge or the prose of the commandments. His world is not a closed one. His own life and the life of mankind are incomplete and he must work toward their perfection.

---

*There were indeed pantheistic trends in the Cabala and Hasidism, but they were kept within bounds by traditional Jewish theism and remained no more than trends.

Chapter VI

THE CHOSEN PEOPLE

T he Problem. What theologians call "the election of Israel," is not just a problem for Jews. From the days of Paul to the present, it has been a matter of concern to Christian thinkers; and it has had a place, though a smaller one, in Muslim teaching as well.

For Christians could not evade the facts: Jesus of Nazareth appeared and worked within the framework of Jewish life; Christianity grew out of Judaism and based itself on the Hebrew Scriptures. As a result, Christian thinkers tended to divide into two groups. One held that the Jews had been the chosen people of God, but forfeited their chosenness by making the golden calf, and later by rejecting Jesus. The other group, following Paul, held that the failures of Israel had not completely destroyed their special relation to God. There was a deep mystery here, and ultimately there would be a reconciliation. The outcome of such theories was that the leaders of Christianity never decreed extermination upon the Jews. They tolerated and even indicted massacres, persecutions, expulsions, and vilifications; but in the otherwise monolithic Christianity of medieval Europe, some kind of place had to be allotted to Jews and Judaism.

Islam, which drew much of its doctrine and lore from Jewish sources, recognized the Jewish and Christian revelations as basically authentic—as stages on the road to the final and perfect revelation through Muhammad. Jews and Christians, the peoples of the Book, were therefore generally tolerated, but assigned an inferior status.

I am not aware of any serious discussion of these matters in present-day Islam. But Christians have been engaged in considerable rethinking of the subject. The best publicized instance is that of the Second Vatican Council, which led to a cautious (and from the Jewish standpoint, far from adequate) though no doubt well-meant pronouncement. Many Protestants and certain individual Catholics have gone much further; the writings of James Parkes and Reinhold Niebuhr on the subject are outstanding. (Some Christian philo-Semites exceed Jewish writers in their estimate of Jewish virtues and their expectations of Jewish performance.)

But this belief in the special role of the Jewish people within the divine economy, which is firmly held by many Christians, is a source of embarrassment, pain, and perplexity to many Jews.

• **The Background.**   The belief had gone unchallenged among Jews throughout the centuries. It is plainly expressed in passage after passage in the Bible, and constantly recurs in the traditional prayerbook. When the scroll of the Torah is read in the synagogue, each person who is called up for the reading praises the God "who has chosen us from among all peoples and given us His law." Closely allied are a series of benedictions containing the formula "who has sanctified us by His commandments and commanded us—followed by a reference to the specific rite to be performed. Without multiplying quotations, to show the presence—indeed the ubiquitousness —of the doctrine in the standard sources, we must take note, however, of the character of the teaching.

First, there is no suggestion that the choice of Israel implies an inherent "racial" superiority. Deuteronomy reminds the Israelites that they were not chosen because they were numerous —"you are the smallest of peoples"—and that they were to receive the promised land for no virtue of their own (Deuteronomy 7:7, 9:4–6). Nor are they to regard themselves as specially talented: it will be by observing God's laws, and thus only, that they will gain a reputation for wisdom (Deuteronomy 4:16 ff.).

This brings us to a second point. The election of Israel is not for world conquest; it confers no rights and privileges, but rather duties. Israel has been chosen to obey the law. This is the constant burden of the biblical writers; it is also characteristic of traditional prayers and benedictions. The prophet Amos insists that just because of the special care which God has given Israel, He will punish them more severely for disobedience and faithlessness (Amos 3:2).[27]

Third, while one may find chauvinistic utterances in the Bible, as in all national literatures of the past and present, there is a frequent suggestion that the choice of Israel is for the ultimate benefit and blessing of all men. Isaiah's great vision of a warless world—something new and revolutionary in human thought—includes the expectation that divine guidance for all peoples will issue from Zion. Indeed, it is precisely this guidance which will make peace possible (Isaiah 2:1 ff.). The great prophet of the exile depicts the people of Israel as the servant of the Lord, through whose suffering other peoples will be healed, and as a "light of the nations" through whom God will bring His salvation to the ends of the earth (Isaiah 53:5, 49:6).[28]

Perhaps more impressive than these visionary utterances is the evidence in the Bible itself for a missionary movement which won many new adherents to Judaism. This movement declined after a while, but in the last centuries before the Christian era it revived with tremendous energy, and it continued for centuries until it was brought to a stop by the political power of Christianized Rome.[29]

• **Shifting Positions.** But despite all these considerations, a good many modern Jews have been unhappy about the idea. Some, no doubt, feared Gentile disapproval of what might seem to be Jewish arrogance. Others were genuinely troubled by a concept that seemed to them both irrational and presumptuous. Another factor was the rise of a Zionist movement which was understood by many (though by no means all) of its adherents as completely secular. They were interested in the "normalization" of Jewish life through the establishment of a Jewish state; for, they argued, the Jews are different from other peoples only in that they do not presently have a land and government of their own. And since the Reform movement of the nineteenth century was predominantly anti-Zionist, and this movement had laid great stress on the "mission of Israel" to bring prophetic monotheism to the world, many of the nationalists were all the more disposed to discard the notion of a unique spiritual role for their people. ,(Yet there were others who argued that the prophetic ideals could be made effective in the world only if they were incorporated in the legal and social order of a Jewish national state).[30]

Today there is a wide variation among thinking and believing Jews on this subject. The orthodox believe without question in the election of the Jewish people, since it is taught unequivocally in the Bible. Many others, not fundamentalists, are still deeply impressed both by the biblical statements and by the character of Jewish history. Most extreme is Will Herberg, with his flat assertion that the Jews are a supernatural people.[31] And Arthur A. Cohen has moved in the same direction with a book entitled *The Natural and the Supernatural Jew.*

Such assertions are almost impossible to discuss. It is extremely difficult, to say the least, to explain what is meant by "a supernatural people." And even were we to agree on a definition, one is at a loss to find a way of proving that any people is or is not supernatural.

At the other extreme, Mordecai M. Kaplan has completely rejected the idea of a chosen people; and this notion has been systematically eliminated from the prayerbook of the Reconstructionist movement, which Dr. Kaplan founded. In contrast with Herberg's position, that of Kaplan can be readily articulated. It regards as impertinence and self-delusion the supposition that the universe is critically concerned about the denizens of a small satellite of one of the lesser stars. Still more unacceptable to Kaplan is the notion that among the inhabitants of that planet, one little people has been singled out by Divinity for a central, perhaps even a cosmic role. Such a claim, he holds, is both foolish and arrogant. It is difficult to answer this criticism in logical terms. But if logic is on Kaplan's side, facts seem to be against him.

Kaplan is prepared to admit that the Jews have a "vocation"; all peoples have their several vocations.[32] But the real issue is not one of terminology: it is the character of the reality to which the terms point. The phenomenon of the Jewish people is the same whether we say that it was "chosen" or just "called."

To speak of the vocation of a people is to use an analogy from the life of individuals. But not every man has a vocation. Some just have a job, others are unemployed. (Of course, in both groups there are some persons who have a vocation which circumstances prevent them from following.) What distinguishes a job from a calling is not, to my mind, the honor and prestige that attach to some kinds of work and are not accorded to others. It is rather to be found in the attitude of the worker toward his work. The most humble task—according to the world's valuation—is a calling if the laborer finds satisfaction in it and feels he is rendering a useful service.

But there are plenty of people, not bad people, who have no special aptitude, no special energy or eagerness; they do what they must, and no more. Either they have no vocation or they have not yet found theirs. Their own work may be useful to society, but they get no particular satisfaction from what they contribute or from the quality of their performance. This is said without condescension or contempt. There are many routine jobs in our world which, though necessary to the smooth running of our economy, are not calculated to fire the imagination of those who perform them. The prevailing standards of "success" do little to reveal the possibilities of vocation in a job that offers neither wealth, power, nor publicity. One of our unsolved problems is to convince ourselves that there is dignity in any useful work honestly performed. But though many of the current distinctions are arbitrary and artificial, there is probably no way to avoid giving special dignity (and perhaps we should not try to avoid it) to those kinds of work that require high degrees of skill, long training, or rare and unusual talent. The same applies to those callings that involve extensive and heavy responsibilities.

As among individuals, so among peoples there is a wide variety. Some have played a prominent role in world history, and some have not. It is not prejudice to say that the roles of the Ammonites, the Afghans, the Paraguayans, and the Montenegrins in human civilization and culture are not comparable to those of the Phoenicians, the Hindus, the Mexicans, and the Greeks. It is also worth noting that many peoples who have made outstanding contributions in past millennia have ceased to exist or have become unproductive; and we do not know when other nations whose historic part has hitherto been modest—or who are just now emerging as nations—will advance to the center of the stage.

Jewish history, however, presents a special complex of problems to the thoughtful student. Here is a people that has played a significant part in world history through thousands of years. Unlike the ancient Egyptians and the ancient and modern Chinese, this people did not owe its continued existence to the possession of a fertile and well-protected country. For most of the past two thousand years they had no territory of their own. Yet despite small numbers, total powerlessness, and dispersion, they have been important in world history both for what they have done and for what has been done to them. Their ordeal and their contribution have been extraordinary. There is literally no parallel or analogue to the history of the Jews. Let the professors of history name one.

To all this the enemies of Israel give eloquent testimony. Without reviewing the ghastly tale of violence, humiliation, oppression, and massacre in earlier centuries, one must be awed at the magnitude and intensity of the obsession which in modern times we call anti-Semitism. Why have both the extreme right and the extreme left been driven to such convulsive efforts to exterminate this one small group? Why did the Nazis have to carry on the "final solution" even to the detriment of their own war effort? What has caused the Soviet leaders to encourage the Arab nations to finish the job in the present? One hardly knows which is more incredible: the persistence of the Jewish people through three thousand difficult years, or the untiring efforts of the Gentile world to liquidate them.

As Jewish existence presents a problem to the outsider—be he hostile or sympathetic—so it confronts the Jew himself with many perplexities. A great amount of energy has been expended by modern Jews on the attempt to define and classify the Jewish people. Is Jewish identity racial, national, or religious? The facts do not accommodate themselves to any of the usual classifications.

Thus, even if we abandon the language of chosenness, and accept Dr. Kaplan's terminology of vocation, we have not escaped from the predicament that distresses him. Granted that every people has its own vocation—and this assumption is still to be proved—the facts indicate that the Jewish people has a special vocation.

• **Still Chosen?**   But one may ask: Do the considerations thus far advanced lead to any theological conclusion? Or is this all a matter of historical circumstance, even doom? What connection, if any, is there between the biblical Israel and the Jews of today? Are the latter really the lineal heirs of the prophets? Many Christian theologians have argued through the centuries that the Jews, once chosen, are chosen no more; they have forfeited their distinction, and the Church is now the true Israel. Even if we disregard this invidious view, it can still be argued that Israel accomplished its "mission" when it gave the world the Bible with its message of ethical monotheism. Why need the people of Israel continue, and what further claim does it have to being special?

Or the matter might be put thus: As long as Jews believed that the Torah was literally the word of God, and that He had given it to Israel, the idea of a chosen people made sense. And it found expression in the conscientious fulfillment of the commandments by the overwhelming majority of Jews. But today the religious life of the Jewish people is in a state of chaos. A considerable proportion of today's Jews have explicitly or implicitly rejected all positive religion. Of those who maintain a tie with the synagogue and with tradition, not a few do so out of mere habit, out of respect for living or dead parents, out of a desire to identify themselves as Jews, but not necessarily as believers. Within the institutions of Jewish religion, one notes a sad amount of materialism, hedonism, ignorance, prayerlessness, and the exploitation of leadership positions for personal advancement. And those who do take their Jewish religion seriously are in many cases searching, questioning, groping in deep uncertainty. Is such a community the chosen of God?

Yet even this problem is not altogether new. Witness the great prophet who was perhaps the first clearly to articulate the doctrine of the "mission of Israel." This is how he describes the "servant of the Lord":

> My chosen one, in whom I delight,
> I have put My spirit upon him,
> He shall teach the true way to the nations. . .
> I created you, and appointed you
> A covenant-people, a light of nations. . .(Isaiah 42:1, 6)

And yet in the very same chapter, the prophet depicts God as complaining:

> Who is so blind as My servant,
> So deaf as the messenger I send? (Isaiah 42:19)

There has always been a tragic disparity between what the Jewish people is and what the Jewish people might be—a specific instance of a universal human tragedy.

Still, even in the spiritual chaos of our time there is much of a positive nature to be said about contemporary Jewry. It has manifested enormous creative energy in innumerable fields: industrial, academic, scientific, artistic, literary, and particularly in areas concerned with human welfare. This creative energy was inhibited neither by the horrors of the 1930s nor the affluence of the 1950s and beyond. The Jews have been prominently identified with liberal and progressive causes in North America. In the recent struggle for the rights of black Americans, a disproportionately high percentage of whites who involved themselves were Jewish. (In due course, extremist black leaders got rid of them.) And this happened at a time when Jews had come to feel secure, and did not need the support of liberal forces for their own benefit.

Little short of miraculous is the revival of Jewish consciousness and self-identification among the Jews of the Soviet Union, who for half a century had been denied the opportunity to learn about their own past, and had been cut off from meaningful ties with the Jews of other lands. No one had foreseen that thousands among them would demand, still less obtain, permission to emigrate to Israel. And in the Americas, despite a great increase in the rate of mixed marriage, Jewish self-identification is still high, and the response to Jewish need— especially the plight of the State of Israel—is extraordinary.

In the State of Israel, despite a chronic military and economic crisis, the inequalities of status and opportunity between oriental and European Jews have led not only to deep heart-searching, but to constructive government action. Many Israelis, too, have been troubled by what they considered injustices to Arabs inside and outside their borders. I have not heard of any public protest in Arab countries against the cruelty toward their Jewish citizens, and there have been few voices speaking for moderation and peace.

And indeed, whatever faults may be found with the Jews, individually and collectively, their enemies have made them look good. To list anti-Semitic individuals and societies is to list the enemies of freedom, reason, and humanity. Wherever human liberty and dignity have been denied—whether in the name of blood and soil, dialectic materialism, or law and order —the Jew has been singled out for special attack. He has the unfortunate, but honorable fate to be hated by all tyrants, both of the right and the left.

Thus the unique role of the Jewish people in history is not entirely a matter of choice. Even those Jews who would like to disassociate themselves from the religion and destiny of their ancestors find themselves somehow caught up in both. The prophet Ezekiel put the truth brutally: "What you have in mind shall never come to pass—when you say, 'We will be like the nations, like the families of the lands, worshiping wood and stone.' As I live—declares the Lord God—I will reign over you with a strong hand and with an outstretched arm and with overflowing fury" (Ezekiel 20:32-33). Of course, this grim warning does not threaten those who embrace their Jewish identity with love.

That the Jewish people have a special role in the divine economy is ultimately a matter of faith, as are all the other affirmations of religion. But the realities of Jewish life in the past and present seem to bolster and justify that faith.

Chapter VII

THE EXODUS: EVENT AND IDEA

Event. The intimate connection between Jewish corporate existence and universal human concerns which we have been discussing appears in a striking fashion in the exodus from Egypt—which marks at once the beginning of Jewish nationhood and, as we shall see, the beginning of the redemption of mankind.

But did the Exodus ever happen? It is ironic that the oldest known reference to the people of Israel is an announcement that they have ceased to exist. An Egyptian monument set up 1,230 years before the Christian era asserts, "Israel is laid waste, his seed is not." But this highly premature declaration is the only mention of Israel found in old Egyptian sources. No record has been unearthed on stone or papyrus of Hebrew slaves in Egypt, or of their departure from the land.

The silence of the Egyptian sources, and the miraculous elements in the biblical account, have led some to wonder whether there ever was an Egyptian bondage, a Moses, or an Exodus. Yet all serious historians agree that at least some of the Hebrew tribes lived in Egypt and were oppressed there, and that they made their escape under the leadership of a great man; moreover, their freedom was assured when a military force pursuing them was caught and drowned in a marshy area of the Suez.

That the Exodus was a historical event is attested by a number of small details. Moses, Aaron, and Phinehas are Egyptian names. The cities built by the Hebrew slaves are mentioned in the Bible by the old names they bore in the probable time of the Exodus, not by the very different names they had at the time when the Bible story was written down.

But there is a broader consideration that seems even more decisive. We understand why the kings of Ethiopia traced their descent back to Solomon, or why the imperial family of Japan formerly claimed to be the offspring of the sun god. But would any people invent the tale that their ancestors were slaves? We may therefore be certain that the oppression and the liberation actually happened, even though later generations exaggerated the numbers involved, and adorned the incident with all sorts of marvels.

• **Idea.** But the importance of any historical event lies not only in what happened, but in the meaning which the happenings acquired, in the continuing impact of the event on minds and hearts. However small the number of slaves that escaped from Egypt with Moses—an incident not apparently deemed worth recording by Egyptian officialdom—to the biblical authors it was the commanding event of history. They refer to it constantly. The Ten Commandments begin with the affirmation, "I the Lord am your God who brought you out of the land of Egypt" (Exodus 20:2). And one version of the fourth commandment runs "Remember that you were a slave in Egypt, and the Lord your God freed you from there with a mighty hand and an outstretched arm; therefore the Lord your God commanded you to observe the sabbath day" (Deuteronomy 5:15). The Israelites are repeatedly instructed to tell their children the story of the deliverance (Exodus 10:2, 13:8, 13:14 ff.; Deuteronomy 6:20 ff.). The building of Solomon's temple was begun in the 480th year after the Exodus (I Kings 6:1). The prophets frequently refer to the deliverance from Egypt as a signal evidence of God's love (e.g., Hosea 1:1, Amos 2:10), and a number of psalms rehearse the story in poetic form (77, 78, 105, 106, 114, 135, 136).

It is small wonder, then, that wherever the Bible was read or its stories retold, the Exodus held enormous meaning for those who struggled or yearned for freedom. During the American Revolution, patriot preachers constantly compared George III to Pharaoh and George Washington to Moses. And the hopes of the black slave in America were expressed in the poignant spiritual "Go Down, Moses."

All the more was the Exodus the central point of history in Jewish life and observance. At every morning and evening service of the synagogue, the _Shema_—the affirmation of God's unity—is followed by a section that refers to the Exodus, and reaches its climax in words from the song of deliverance at the Sea. The section then concludes by praising God as the Redeemer of Israel in the past and the future. In the prayer of sanctification (_kiddush_) which introduces the sabbath and festivals, these occasions are described as "a memorial of our going forth out of Egypt." This applies also to holy days, such as the New Year and the Feast of Weeks, which are not traditionally connected with the Exodus. Finally, the most notable family celebration in each year is the Seder service and meal on the eve of Passover, which includes the ringing statement: "Every man in every generation must regard himself as having been delivered from Egypt."

Here we come to the heart of the matter. The Exodus is not a mere event out of the dim past, but an experience which each generation must relive. Why is it so important?

• **Hope.** The modern term "power structure" can be applied most appropriately to ancient Egypt. That rich, powerful, culturally advanced society was highly organized; it may be fittingly viewed as a pyramid whose broad base consisted of slaves from many lands, with the Pharaoh at the pinnacle. He was both head of the earthly establishment and visible representative of the heavenly establishment. He was not merely an absolute monarch, he was an incarnate god. Power was deity, deity was power. (Other ancient peoples had very similar views.)

But the Exodus, for those who experienced it, meant that God is on the side of the weak and downtrodden. He identifies Himself not with those who conquer territory for Him, who rear

Him massive temples and provide Him with lavish sacrifices, but with those who need Him most, who have no hope but Him. That was a revolutionary concept. Throughout all succeeding ages men remembered: It once happened that the weak, the helpless, the slaves, the strangers won a victory. Such a victory seemed to them against the rules of nature, which always give the prize to the strong, or to the craftily ruthless. Such a victory, they declared, could be nothing short of a miracle, a breakthrough of the divine into the mechanism of affairs. And if it happened once, it can happen again. The hope of a world redeemed grows out of the memory of Israel redeemed from Egypt—an event to be relived in each generation.

Or we may restate the idea thus: Science is for the most part an interpretation of physical reality in mechanistic terms. Technology, whatever its avowed aims, is too often the mechanization of human life. It compels man to adapt himself to the machine, when it should be the other way around. And people ask, often in desperation: Is the world nothing but machinery? Am I myself no more than a machine, to be flung aside when broken, worn out, or obsolescent? Am I even less than that, a mere component of a big machine, with no independent existence of my own?

To such questions the memory of the Exodus provides an answer. It tells that an efficient industrial-military complex failed to keep slaves in bondage. It speaks of men, divinely led, who regained their liberty and reaffirmed their humanity. It has happened, therefore it can happen. We need not be slaves of the machine. For God is not only supreme power, He is above all supreme goodness.

Such convictions were complete certainties to the many generations who regarded the biblical story of the Exodus, with all its miraculous details, as factual beyond all doubt. We of today cannot be quite that sure. Even though the basic elements of the story—the enslavement of the Hebrews and their eventual flight to liberty—are almost surely historical, we cannot demonstrate that these events were the result of divine intervention. The victory of the weak might be no more than a minor accident. The interpretation Jews have put on these events, we admit frankly, is an expression of faith. But it is a faith made the more impressive by the rich moral and spiritual implications that follow from it.

Moreover, the universal bearing of the Jewish people's experience is made manifest and explicit in the interpretation of the Exodus. It seems to be no accident that the ritual for Passover eve says, "Every man in every generation must regard himself as having been delivered from Egypt"—it does not say "every Jew" but "every man." No people is finally redeemed until all peoples are redeemed.

Chapter VIII

RELIGION IN ACTION

The preceding chapters have treated questions that are predominantly questions of belief, questions more or less speculative and theoretical. But all of them have implications for religious living, in terms both of mood and of specific actions. Perhaps this is true of theology in general, rooted as it is in a faith anterior to our reasoning. It is certainly true of Judaism, the creedal elements of which are so largely left implicit in laws and commandments. And our exploratory approach, which evaluates theological concepts not only by their rational validity, but also by their moral consequences, has intensified this consideration.

By the same token, when we turn to examine some of the practical aspects of religious living, we shall never be far from theological principles. The insight and the resolve, the conviction and the commandment, cannot be separated.

• **Three Kinds of Religion.** We apply the term religion to a complex phenomenon, which includes many elements: intellectual, emotional, social, ethical, legal, ceremonial. These elements are combined in many different ways and proportions, but there are at least three patterns that appear repeatedly and which we may designate as three kinds of religion. Probably none of them exists in absolutely pure form without some admixture of the others.

One is the religion of security. It is manifested in simple faith and trust, submission and conformity. (These words are here used descriptively, not for praise or blame.) The individual is fortified against the shocks, pains, and sorrows of his life by the assurance that all is well; that the shocks and sufferings are transitory, unimportant, even beneficial; and that ultimate reward and bliss will be the lot of the steadfast. Such assurances make present pain more tolerable and enable the believer not only to survive, but to live bravely, cheerfully, and even productively.

A second type is the religion of excitement. Here a broad preliminary statement is necessary. Man has a need, not always clearly conscious and articulate, but insistent, to feel that his life is significant. In the absence of other sources for such meaning, physical and emotional excitement provide a temporary illusion of meaningfulness. To this end individuals utilize alcohol and drugs, gambling, daredevil driving and other means of courting physical danger, amorous adventure, and so on. (Not all escapism is of this sort. Alcohol and other drugs tend to become narcotic rather than exhilarating, and chronic television-watchers are stupefied rather than stimulated by the tube.) Conflict may be painful and frightening, but it is not boring. A man may have been harboring suicidal thoughts, but if someone assaults him, he will resist desperately, and while the fight lasts, he will not question the value of life. The end of a war has meant a letdown for many soldiers who had never felt so intensely alive as in hand-to-hand combat.

Not all kinds of excitement are so destructive and barren as those we have mentioned. Athletic competition provides both participants and spectators with excitement that is usually harmless. Many activities that are inherently meaningful—for instance, creative work in science and the arts—may be accompanied by emotional tensions that heighten the experience. Nor are the delights of the senses to be rejected in contempt or condemnation. The point is simply that our sense of aliveness and significance is intensified by excitement, even if the latter is generated artificially.

In the practice of religion one may also find instances of such a buildup and release of emotional tension. At certain festivals of the Aztecs, a captive or slave was brought before the assembled multitude, and a priest cut the victim's heart out of the living body as a sacrifice to the gods. We may think such an act horrible, especially as an expression of religious feeling, but we cannot doubt that it gave the onlookers an enormous emotional kick. The bullfight is not so very different, and it too originated in ancient religious rites. But religion can also provide emotional catharsis without cruelty. The dances of the dervishes, the extravagances of pentecostal sects, the frenzy of the old-fashioned camp meeting, and the ecstatic celebrations of the Hasidim are instances. Even the more conventional and restrained religious groups have their moments of excitement. One feels it in so orderly a milieu as the Reform synagogue, in the New Year service just before the ram's horn is sounded, or on Atonement eve as the singing of Kol Nidre begins. In mystical religions, the quest for security and the quest for excitement are often combined.

The third type of religion may be characterized as the religion of duty. It lays primary stress not on what the worshiper feels, but upon what he does. It sets up requirements, sometimes in broad ideals and principles, sometimes in specific and detailed commandments, for the individual, the family, and the community. The fulfillment of such requirements may be accompanied by a sense of security and tranquillity, or by a mood of tension and excitement. But the deed is the central thing, the associated emotions are something additional, though they may be precious.

The three aspects are combined in most, if not all, historical religions; the proportions in the mix vary not only from religion to religion, but from sect to sect, locality to locality, and time to time. And depending on the proportions, the result may be wholesome or the reverse. One thinks, for example, of the excessive emphasis on inner security in Christian Science. On the other hand, dramatic devotions and sermons on the crucifixion have too often sent excited crowds from the church to the Jewish quarter, to massacre and rob those allegedly responsible for the death of the savior. In our own day, chemical shortcuts to supernal bliss have been offered the unwary, sometimes with tragic, even fatal results.

In all true biblical religion, the element of personal and communal discipline is central.

● **The Religious Person.**   We have noted three general kinds of religion, but it is not appropriate to classify religious persons (or religious personalities) in the same fashion. People express their religious attitudes in a great variety of ways and through many different instrumentalities. But first we may ask what in general is meant by the term "a religious person"? Perhaps the one characteristic which all such individuals have in common is sincerity, a reasonable congruence between belief and conduct.

Sincerity—one cannot overemphasize this—is a goal, not a possession. Religious people, like all people, are imperfect. Religious people, like all people, do not consistently live up to their professions.

The charge of hypocrisy is too often made lightly and unfairly. The hypocrite makes a deliberate pretense to virtue and piety, when he is not virtuous or pious and does not want to be. Most people, however, live more or less contradictory lives. This is often because they are unable to recognize the contradictions. Generations of pious folk practiced chattel slavery without realizing that they were thereby negating the basic principles of their religion. (They were the more protected because old custom, rooted in Scripture, had legitimized slavery.) But people often do the wrong thing when they know better. This universal fact of human existence is not an excuse for the sinful churchgoer, but it is not in itself a reason to denounce him as a hypocrite. The truly religious person is the one who tries hard to make his conduct consistent with his avowed beliefs and principles, even though he does not fully succeed.

Nevertheless, consistency of faith and act, detached from all other considerations, is not enough to justify our calling someone religious. We should hardly apply the term to one whose god is Money, and whose devotion to that deity is unswerving. The religious person recognizes a value or values that transcend him. He belongs to something or Someone greater than himself. He offers himself to be used by that in which he believes, not the reverse. In the deepest and truest sense, a religious person is humble.

• **The Kinds of Religious People.** We spoke above about the religion of security, the religion of excitement, and the religion of duty. But it is probable that all religious persons derive security from their faith, though in at least two different ways. There are some whose religion is a cocoon that insulates them from the painful realities of the world, especially from those realities that do not afflict them personally at the moment. There are others whose faith enables them to keep their equilibrium in the midst of the unsettling experiences of daily life, and to deal courageously, productively, and compassionately with their own problems and those of others.

Some find security through a well-articulated theology, a clearly defined creed. Others leave their concepts of reality implicit or even confused, and draw strength from some kind of discipline—personal prayer, ceremonial observance, the performance of ethical duties, even the mechanics of a congregation. (Someone has to handle finances, keep the building in repair, and usher at services; these tasks too can be fulfilling.)

Probably the simplest classification of religious people is into those who stress authority and those who stress freedom in religious life, between orthodox and liberal religionists. Each of these approaches has its own advantage. The liberal practices his faith in freedom, which for him is a self-justifying value. The orthodox who subjects his thought and conduct to authority derives thereby a degree of certainty which the liberal—who relies more on his own intelligence and knows its limitations—cannot attain.

Each of these approaches has its own typical weakness, its besetting sin, so to speak. Liberalism is likely to become casual and superficial. The liberal, rightly according to his views, takes into consideration the intellectual and social developments of his age. But too often this means that he substitutes current fashions for his historical faith, or glibly identifies new notions with the old religion—when he should more seriously and critically inquire whether in fact his inherited religious position should correct, modify, or deepen the new discoveries and insights.

The besetting sin of orthodoxy is a well-camouflaged pride. This may seem strange; for some orthodoxies condemn as "intellectual pride" the persistent questionings of those who are not satisfied with traditional dogmas and rules. But in fact the individual who challenges accepted notions, not out of cussedness and frivolity, but because he is devoted to the truth, is often more humble than one who professes to subject his mind to the control of a church, book, or tradition. For the fundamentalist knows he is right! Of course, it is not he personally who is right, but the Bible, the religious code, the church. Yet it is this submission to authority that gives him the stamina to judge, condemn, even persecute those who question the authority he accepts.

It is only in recent years that there has been a serious attempt at dialogue between fundamentalists and modernists. Such exchange of ideas may be helpful in guarding liberal religion from shallowness and orthodox religion from arrogance.

• **Ethics and Religion.**   Virtually all the religions of today agree that ethical conduct is one of the basic demands of religious commitment. The old orthodoxies are today less isolated than formerly; in our cosmopolitan society, where persons of such varied religious backgrounds are in frequent contact with each other, even those who lay primary emphasis on their specific dogma or rite are constrained to acknowledge and respect the probity and moral excellence of persons outside their community. And in liberal religion there has been a strong tendency to identify the ethical and the religious. Is there then any difference between the moral man and the religious man? Can one be religious and immoral? And what shall we say of the person who claims to be irreligious and yet lives by high ethical standards?

First, a moral position can be based on purely prudential considerations. Epicurus asserted that pleasure was the highest value, but he did not advise people to become epicures. For he held that self-indulgence leads to many pains, and therefore counseled a regimen of moderation. Somewhat similar was the outlook of Aristotle. His study of man's nature led him to conclude that man's unique gift is the power of reason; therefore the exercise of reason brings him true happiness. Such a fulfillment, however, is possible only if one learns to control his appetites and emotions and to follow the golden mean in all things. So there can be an ethic of enlightened selfishness. It may be less than sublime, but it's an ethic.

Second, the outwardly pious scoundrel and the saintly athiest do exist; but if they constitute a problem, it is not difficult to find answers to it.

As for the person who is devout in church or punctilious about ritual observance, but immoral in his daily life, we say that his religion is either stupid and uninformed, or it is insincere. His behavior is regrettable, it is a "profanation of the Name of God," but it does not prove that religion is either bad or useless.

Of the saintly atheist, we may suspect that he is living on inherited capital. He has retained the ethical implications of biblical faith while rejecting their theological underpinning. Cut flowers can be beautiful for a while, but they produce no new plants to bear flowers in turn; for that, roots are needed. As a matter of experience, the decline of the churches and the increase of violence and brutality seem to have gone hand in hand; and the rebellious young idealists of our time have in large measure turned to some kind of religious faith, even if it was an unconventional one, preferably different from that of their parents.

But if the morality of the atheist is more than inheritance and habit, if he himself is passionately committed to righteousness, then—as we have seen—he is affirming something superhuman, something cosmically valid. However negative his language, he has dedicated his life to the divine.

• **Once More, the Heart and the Mind.**   Our time has seen a resurgence of unhealthy emotionalism. Something of that sort was inevitable; it was a response to a need. Both the excessive rationalism of the scientific revolution and the mechanization and depersonalization of life caused by the technological revolution were bound to evoke a reaction. The value of the individual, the claim of the heart, the importance of gentle humanity needed reaffirmation. In many cases, all this has taken the form of religious revival.

But a thoughtful person is bound to be distressed by many of the gooey, sentimental-cum-sensual expressions of contemporary religion. A shortcut to God has been sought through drugs. Young people play at being Orientals, and prate about Krishna-consciousness and Zen without making a real effort to understand the religions of the Far East. Newly awakened young Christians go about with copies of the King James version of the Bible in hand, eager to prove Christian doctrine from the "Old Testament," unaware that many fundamentalists (to say nothing of liberal Christians) no longer believe that these "proof texts" prove anything. The same trend has produced at least two successful musical entertainments, later made into films, in which the Christian doctrine of love is thoroughly intertwined with slanderous and inflammatory depiction of "the Jews." (That Jews have been entrepreneurs of this project only points up the irrationality of it all.) The assault on reason has even taken the form of ventures into witchcraft by people who know better and are deliberately and with malice aforethought rejecting their own intelligence.

Of course, the heart has its reasons which the reason does not know. The Stoic attempt to repress all emotion was not only futile, but in a sense antihuman. We need to acknowledge our emotions and to give expression to them. It is important for us not only to love and be loved, but to say that we love and to be told that we are loved. But the assumption that spontaneous feeling is a better guide of conduct than intelligent thought is refuted by all human experience. There is a certain place in life for the sudden impulse, the "hunch" we feel and cannot justify, the faith that flies in the face of facts and of prudence. But the odds are long against any wager we make without reflection. Once in a while a hunch pays off; most of the time it proves an illusion. Cold intellect is not infallible, but the warm undisciplined heart is even more likely to err.

● **Love Supreme.** These preceding remarks were a necessary introduction to discourse on love, which everyone talks about nowadays. From rock singers to theologians, they all hymn love, and it has become at times a little hard to distinguish the rock singers from the theologians: for the former are inclined to preach on occasion, and the latter no longer distinguish so sharply between spirit and flesh.

It has, moreover, been a favorite sport for nineteen centuries to contrast Judaism, the religion of stern, cruel justice with Christianity, the religion of warm, generous love. In fact, the idea of a loving God, and the commandment to love God and one's neighbor, are clearly expressed in the Bible, the Christians borrowed them from Judaism. But this statement might be taken to mean that Judaism anticipated Christianity in affirming the higher morality of love. And that might imply that justice and love are in some sense opposites, and that the religion of love is superior to the religion of justice. In fact, the two things go hand in hand, and justice is the primary ingredient in the mix.

● **The Boundaries of Justice and Love.** It is not easy to draw a line of demarcation between justice and love. Justice, as expounded in Jewish sources, is not cruel and vengeful, and it is not a matter of following the rule book mechanically. Justice requires us to be kind, for people have a right to humane and considerate treatment. Thus, while the Bible repeatedly urges us to be generous to the poor, it did not leave the needy dependent on the sympathy of individuals. It assigned part of the annual harvest to the poor as their right. Three thousand years ago, Judaism recognized what Western civilization has admitted only in late years: that the destitute and deprived have a claim on the society and the economy. There can be no justice without human warmth. And yet the Bible forbids a judge to decide a lawsuit in favor of a poor man unless his claim is a valid one. To award him something to which he is not entitled, just because we feel sorry for him, would not be true compassion; we should thereby encourage him to use his poverty as a means of taking an advantage of someone else. Similarly, a parent who will not intervene to prevent his child from bullying another because he can't bear to see his own youngster cry is not displaying love.

Real love cannot abide injustice, and real justice is not unloving.

What, then, is the difference? Part of our difficulty in answering the question is that we use the word "love" in so many different senses—sexual, romantic, sentimental, moral, cosmic and in innumerable combinations of these elements. To utter the word "love" makes us feel good, it does not convey any clear meaning.

The basic difference, I suggest, is not between sternness and generosity, or between rigidity and flexibility; it is to be found in another direction. By justice we ordinarily mean a standard of conduct adopted by society because it is beneficial to society; by love we mean something more personal, subjective, and spontaneous.[33]

It was the apostle Paul who saw these two things as antithetical. He found it frustrating and depressing to struggle to obey the Law, even the moral law embodied in the Ten Commandments. He therefore sought to base religion on inner emotion, arguing: If your heart is right, you will do all the right things spontaneously and effortlessly. Instead of trying to obey the law and failing, you will be fulfilling your own redeemed nature.

This is a sketchy and incomplete account of Paul's viewpoint, which one can respect even if one does not accept it. But it has now become popular in a crude secularized form, which does not seem worthy of respect at all. This latter may be suggested by the following personal experience:

I used to call on an invalid who was full of bitterness and hostility. She would greet me, "You only come out of a sense of duty, but I want you to come just because you love me." This suggests that an act is somehow unworthy if you do it because you think you ought to; what really counts is what you do because you feel like doing it. Should I then have stayed away from this person until I felt the irresistible desire to listen to her complaints, or should I have felt guilty for not having such a desire? I do not believe so.

This small incident points toward a broad generalization. We need norms and standards. We must accept discipline. It should be largely self-discipline, but it must be rooted in something more solid and dependable than personal inclination. Affection is more likely to be the result of responsible conduct than the cause of personal righteousness, let alone social righteousness. Before we can attain the maximum of benevolence and generosity, we must first acquire the minimum of decency and responsibility.

There is probably no age that has heard so much talk of love and compassion, and seen more misery and brutality and violence. And one of the roots of our tragedy is the erosion of simple honesty and integrity in every sphere of our national life.

Never has such stress been laid on the element of love in marriage. Time was when parents arranged matches, with due regard for considerations of money and family; and children obediently married the partners their parents had selected. This appears to us as intolerable tyranny, and no one wants to go back to that system. But the fact that people entered marriage with a sense of obligation gave them some chance to achieve a stability of life within which love might (and often did) flower. Today, the frantic quest for physical and emotional fulfillment, the viewpoint that marriage is an experience rather than a task, has left the family in a shaky state—and people are certainly no happier for the change.

Everyone recognizes that the race problem is one of our most serious and tragic difficulties. There are still some who feel that it can be approached only by a slow educational process designed to eliminate prejudices from men's hearts. But no one has found a method of doing this, and the victims of prejudice cannot wait till it has been devised. What is needed is not that we should all love each other, individually and collectively, but that we should stop wronging each other, individually and collectively. I may not be able to overcome my dislike of an individual or group, even if there is no reason for my dislike, but I can refrain from treating people unjustly. And though the law cannot control my feelings, it can control my behavior.

Some years back, a doctrine of "situation morality" was proposed. Its advocates argued that all ethical codes are limiting and inadequate; even with the Ten Commandments, one could cite cases where obedience would have immoral consequences.

Instead of following rules, we were told, we should examine each situation where a moral choice is necessary, and then do what love requires of us.[34] I do not know to what extent such a formula has been tried out in life. One might safely bet that in "situations" involving sexual conduct, "love" invariably required the fulfillment of present desire. Of course, the "situation" might change later, but it would be comforting to know that at each given moment it was virtuous to do what you wanted to do anyhow.

Actually, the Jewish "legalism" which Christian critics have so often decried, is not as rigid as they have supposed. It recognized that no rule can apply to all circumstances, that changing conditions may affect the application of established principles, and that there are special situations in which regulations must be suspended. But the Jewish legal system did not leave the decision in these ticklish cases to the interested party; it referred him to a scholar whose knowledge and experience qualified him to approve or disapprove some modification or reinterpretation.

Such a procedure, whatever its shortcomings (no question, establishment figures tend to err on the conservative side), still provides more hope of a genuine morality than reliance on mere sentiment. For no matter how deep and genuine love may be, it does not exempt us from having to do things we don't like to do —rather the reverse. The most devoted parent does not spring up with delight if the baby cries at 2 A.M. The most dedicated Olympic athlete does not enjoy every moment of the grueling practice he must complete. We need not adopt the (supposed) Puritan assumption that virtuous conduct is generally disagreeable and that any enjoyable activity is probably a sin. Jewish tradition speaks of the joy found in fulfilling the commandment, but it insists on the performance of the duty, whether the joy is present or not.

If feeling—even the exalted feeling we call love—is an uncertain guide in the practical and tangible issues of human conduct, it is all the more unreliable in the tenuous and abstract area of beliefs. We have all heard about the pitfalls of wishful thinking. A belief, of course, need not be untrue because we find it encouraging and pleasant, but our desire to believe something does not guarantee its credibility. If, as this book contends, we must question even a reasoned, logical conclusion that violates our moral sense, we must certainly scrutinize critically the contentions that mere feeling presents, and check them against the facts and the rules of ordinary reasoning. There is no royal road to virtue or religious truth.

• **About Sin and Guilt.** The notion that guilt feelings are a pathological aberration caused by pressure from without has been much promoted by amateur hedonists and alleged Freudians, but it cannot be seriously sustained. Of course there are people who suffer from exaggerated and neurotic guilt feelings. There are also people who have a phobia about dirt and germs, but no one infers from their behavior that precautions against bacterial infection are unnecessary. Nor does the terror of heights which afflicts some people minimize the reality that one who falls from a high building will be killed. The sense of guilt is pathological when its intensity is out of all proportion to the seriousness of the offense, or when the offense is imaginary.

But the unhappiness we feel at having done wrong or failed to do right is something proper to our human nature. It is not imposed on us by a tyrannical puritanism for such external pressure would only make us discreet in concealing our actions, if something within us did not respond deeply to the sense of our own faults.

A childhood experience will serve to make this plain. My mother had a pretty cover on her dressing table; I got the idea that it would look still prettier if the edge, instead of being straight, were cut in scallops. I decided to surprise her by doing the job, and in my mind's eye saw her calling in the neighbors and displaying my handiwork with pride. Of course the enterprise was a disaster. I wasn't punished and to my mother's baffled inquiry as to why I had cut the cover, I said I didn't know. The contrast between what I had planned to do and what I actually did was so humiliating that I couldn't bear to tell the truth. What we call guilt is not merely the impact of other people's condemnation; it is the outcome of our disappointment with ourselves.

The word "sin" is not fashionable nowadays, but it is indispensable. It indicates another dimension of our moral failure. It is not just a matter of offending others or disappointing ourselves. For righteousness is, we believe, God's will. And when we fall short of righteousness, we fail not only ourselves and our fellows, we fail God as well. That is the force of the term "sin."

A large part of our discomfort with the word may derive from Christian notions that have penetrated deeply into Western culture. For in historical Christianity, sin is viewed not merely as an act or a failure to act, but as a universal human condition. The taint of original sin, like a hereditary sickness, affects all men, and no one can cure himself by his own moral striving. He is a miserable sinner by the very fact of his descent from Adam, before he has committed any act that is subject to moral judgment, and he can escape his sinful condition only through divine intervention.

Buddhism teaches something rather similar, though the formulation and terminology are very different. It holds that man is all but hopelessly tangled in error. As the result of his prior actions, in this and in previous incarnations, he is chained to the unreality and misery of existence. Not only wrongdoing, but any act that affirms life in the ordinary sense, such as marrying and having a family, serves only to increase the weight of the chains that bind him to the wheel of things.

Judaism, however, regards this world neither as an illusion nor as a vale of tears. It is God's world, and we not only may, but should enjoy its delights. But it is not to be exploited selfishly for our amusement alone. We have duties and responsibilities; there are things we ought and ought not do. And being creatures, limited and frail, we do not always adequately fulfill our obligations. Sometimes the cause is forgetfulness, negligence, ignorance, fear, or weakness. Sometimes we deliberately flout God's will. In short, we sin.

Sin, then, is something objective, a specific act or failure to act. It is not a condition, a disease, or an atmosphere. No one is doomed to sin, even though we know that each of us, being human, will sometimes yield to temptation.[35] The healthiest person cannot entirely escape sickness or injury.

This conception is further defined by some common-sense considerations. First, a sinful impulse or intention which is not put into practice is not generally regarded as a sin in Jewish tradition.[36] The Rabbis indeed warn us against sinful thoughts —they apparently are thinking especially of sexual fantasies— and counsel us to concentrate our thoughts on study of the Torah and deeds of righteousness.[37] But one need not belabor his conscience about the inclinations to which he has not yielded.

Second, Judaism does not expect man to achieve superhuman perfection. This despite the stirring challenge, "You shall be holy, for I the Lord your God am holy" (Leviticus 19:1). For this charge does not mean "You must be as holy as I am." It is followed by a whole series of specific enactments, mostly ethical, some ceremonial, by which the Israelites are to practice holiness; and these laws can be fulfilled by ordinary people. Sin is not so much falling short of perfection as falling short of one's own moral potential. Bible and Talmud teach that the greater one's talents, the greater his obligations. But the point was made most dramatically by the Hasidic teacher, Zusya of Manipol, who shortly before his death (in 1S00) remarked: "In the next world, they will not ask me 'Why were you not Moses?' but Why were you not Zusya?'"

Here we find the rationale of that central element in Jewish observance, the Day of Atonement. The Jew confesses his sins and shortcomings, strives to return to God, and endeavors to set his feet again on the right path. Yet he knows that next Yom Kippur he will be back to recite the same prayers again. And still this exercise is neither hypocritical nor futile. We wash our hands, knowing they will get dirty again; we visit the dentist regularly, even though his treatments give us no assurance against new cavities. We are always trying to improve our performance, though we never achieve fully what is within our power.

Finally, as sin is conceived concretely, so is purification from sin. Judaism found it unnecessary to elaborate theories of atonement. It simply urged man to return to God, without speculating as to just how God responds.

Chapter IX ⸺⸺⸺⸺

RELIGION AND THE ARTS

A New Partnership. There has been a great upswing of interest in the arts among religious leaders. We no longer build tired Gothic churches and synthetic Moorish synagogues. Houses of worship erected in recent decades are in a variety of styles, and frequently embody new concepts of the purpose and functions of the religious community. In this endeavor, architects and theologians have worked together. Much new and unconventional liturgical music has been composed, often on commission; rock music has been utilized in worship, and multimedia services have been attempted. Moreover, synagogues and churches have been supporting artistic endeavor as such—the concerts, art shows, and dramatic performances they sponsor are not always limited to explicitly religious themes.

All this is excellent and desirable. The artistic community and the religious community have much to give each other. But they are not, as they may have been once, a single community. Their very cooperation serves to underscore certain problems. Some of these arise in a practical way when a religious institution deals with an artist. What constitutes appropriate artwork for a church, and how much of a budget should be spent on decoration that does not serve a practical purpose? What sort of music is suitable for public worship? Such questions do not lend themselves to easy generalization. An avant-garde architect or composer and a middle-class congregation can probably come to agreement in practice more readily than in theory.

But there are broader questions that we must examine. After all, both religion and the arts are concerned with "spiritual" things. Not infrequently we hear from some pulpits that worship is akin to poetry—a statement that raises questions about the meaning and intent of both. For several generations, too, liberal theologians have compared the inspiration of the prophet (what used to be called "revelation") with that of the creative artist. Such assertions require us to consider carefully the resemblances and differences between religious and artistic endeavor—all the more since for many of our contemporaries art has become a substitute for religion.

• **The Artist as Seer.**   In the classical world, poets were often regarded as inspired seers. The other arts, however, were not thought to be sources of supernal vision, but only skilled crafts. The concept of the poet as visionary seems to have ebbed with the decline of classical culture. In the Middle Ages the religious arts were subject to ecclesiastical control, and secular artistic productions had to please the aristocratic patron who footed the bill. This situation continued to the end of the eighteenth century; even so independent a spirit as Johann Sebastian Bach never doubted that his chief task was to glorify God in accordance with Protestant doctrine—even though he resented the attempts of Leipzig bureaucrats to instruct him in the fulfillment of that task.

Something new emerged in the age of romanticism: the image of the artist as autonomous creator, the bearer of a message, subject to no control but that of his own inspiration. Beethoven saw himself charged with a mission to all humanity. Shelley and Hugo were quite explicit on the subject. Goethe established himself as a potentate of the spirit, though he had taken as his province not only poetry, but science and philosophy as well.

This concept of the artist as seer has survived the romantic period. Mondrian insisted that his painting had metaphysical implications. And theologians today expound not only the scriptures and traditions of their several communities, but also the novels of Dostoevsky and Camus, the poetry of Eliot, the theater of Beckett, and even the canvases of Jackson Pollack.

This may mean only that religious thinkers today recognize

new sources of revelation, which supplement the old ones, and do not necessarily contradict or supersede them. But there is another view which seems to start with Schopenhauer. The gloomy German proposed that we contemplate beauty—in particular, that we listen to music—to relieve the suffering imposed on us by a radically evil existence. Art was to serve as a refuge for a generation that no longer had faith. There are today many persons who seek inner refreshment and renewal, not through personal prayer or public worship, but through going to concerts or listening to records, looking at paintings, and reading good literature.

Does it make any difference by which door we enter the realm of the spirit?

• **Science and Art.** The answer is that in many ways art resembles science more than it does religion.

Science is autonomous. It is based on certain rules of method which must be followed strictly in investigation and explanation. It recognizes no other authority, political, esthetic, moral, or metaphysical. The only value affirmed by science is adherence to its own method. Science as such knows nothing of good or bad, but only of the scientifically valid or invalid. The discoveries of science may be applied to beneficent or to destructive ends; and within the frame of scientific thought there is no norm for distinguishing the useful from the harmful end, and no reason for choosing one more than the other.

Nor is the validity of a scientific hypothesis affected in the slightest by the moral or social character of the person who proposes it. He may be a brute, a traitor, or a heroin dealer, but if his hypothesis is verified by controlled experiment, it is fully established. And saintly character is no guarantee of scientific excellence.

The arts, too, have achieved virtual autonomy. Most artists and critics insist that a work of art is to be judged only by artistic norms. The latter are admittedly not as clear and unequivocal as those of scientific method. The element of personal taste cannot be eliminated, and critical consensus changes with the passing of time. (This too can be overstressed: Homer and the Parthenon, the mosaics of Ravenna and the glass of the Sainte-Chapelle have been consistently admired through the ages; and such recent comers as Shakespeare, Mozart, and Rembrandt seem secure.) But when artistic fashions change, works of art are reevaluated on their artistic merits. The latter may be difficult to define, but they are largely independent of moral and political considerations—except, of course, among the totalitarians. Baudelaire may not be a guide to virtue, but he wrote better poetry than the amiable Longfellow. Wagner was a monster of egoism, ingratitude, and plain dishonesty, and a virulent anti-Semite to boot; but all that does not reduce the magnitude of his musical achievement.

Of course a great work of art may glorify constructive ethical, social, or religious doctrine. Ibsen's *Brand* and Beethoven's *Fidelio* are familiar instances. The greatness of the literature or music enhances the impact of the message, and the sublime intent glorifies the art. But it is not ethical teaching that makes art great. One can find noble sentiments galore in inferior books and plays; and there are extraordinary works of art that are morally neutral or even nihilistic.

• **Religion Makes Demands.**   At this point we see at least one plain difference between science and art on one hand, and biblical religion on the other. The most eloquent and convincing sermon loses its force for us if we know, or think, that the preacher's life does not square with his avowed principles. Many persons have been repelled by organized religion because they found its proponents to be morally deficient or socially insensitive. Those on the outside or the fringes of the churches have perhaps been at times unreasonable and intolerant; the adherents of any religion, being human, will have human frailties. But the critics and dissenters are right in expecting that people who identify themselves with religion should exemplify in a marked degree the moral qualities which religion affirms.

Thus far we have been comparing the creative artist with the spokesman or representative of religion. The contrast is just as striking when we compare the average "consumer" of art and of religion.

Schopenhauer's use of music to escape from the tragedy of life is not essentially different from the use of alcohol or marijuana for the same purpose, though it may be a more refined and less dangerous expedient. Now religion is often utilized for a similar end. People come to public worship frankly seeking calm, relief from tension, and hope in the midst of stress. There is a recognizable parallel between the taut, restless person who tries to get to sleep by repeating the twenty-third Psalm and the insomniac nobleman for whose relief Bach composed the Goldberg Variations.

We have seen, too, that religion may supply not only calm and reassurance, but also the emotional and nervous excitation that humans often crave. Obviously, similar effects can be generated through artistic means. Tension is an essential element in most serious drama; music and dancing can rouse both participants and witnesses to frenzy. The canvases of Van Gogh and di Chirico are "exciting."

It seems to be natural for us sometimes to seek tranquil reassurance, sometimes exaltation and enthusiasm; and all the historical religions provide some measure of response to these needs. But biblical religion, and especially Judaism, adds another basic, indispensable element. Judaism is not only experience, but also commitment. The artistic experience relaxing or exciting, is just experience; it makes no further demands. Perhaps that is why many contemporaries prefer it to the practice of religion. For religion as taught in the Bible is not just the blissful contemplation of the presence of God. It is a discipline of commandments, directed largely to our relationships with other persons, and to our participation in the labors of the community. The most sublime emotion is wasted unless it is expressed in righteous deeds.

There is no intent here to disparage the arts or to minimize their importance. In the foregoing discussion, no account was taken of other values in the artistic experience: the intellectual element, the broadening of horizons, and the sheer enjoyment they provide. But acknowledging all this gratefully, we must also understand that the concert hall and the art museum are not religious sanctuaries and cannot take the place of the latter. The concert hall and art museum offer us much; we accept what we can, and go our way. But the institution of religion offers us much and demands much. That is the irreducible difference.

● **Worship and Poetry.**   Religious thinkers of a liberal stamp have often suggested a kinship between worship and poetry. To deal intelligently with such an assertion, we must first agree on what is meant by poetry. Plainly it is not just a question of meter and rhyme. I suggest the following distinction: In prose the words convey (or should convey) a well-defined meaning, no more, no less. Poetry is a kind of discourse which suggests more than the words themselves clearly mean. However this plus may be accomplished—by rhythm, melody, metaphor, understatement, or some other device—we are made to feel it vibrating around the plain sense of the words.

Now the language of worship, by its very nature, can only be allusive. God cannot be described, still less defined, by human minds and tongues. Whatever we say in prayer is inadequate. But language that at least suggests the mystery and wonder of existence, and the grandeur and love of the God to whom we reach out, is less inadequate than the more precise prose of daily affairs. If, then, the statement that worship is akin to poetry means that by prayer we try to relate ourselves to a Reality beyond our power to envision clearly, and that we employ the language of metaphor to reduce a little the gap between God and man, no one is likely to disagree.

But one cannot escape the feeling that, for some of our contemporaries, worship is no more than an esthetic experience. It seems designed to awaken in us, imaginatively and dramatically, the kind of emotions once felt by those who really believed in a living God. The use of Hasidic tunes and dances in liberal synagogues seems to be a case in point—an attempt to evoke the mood of Hasidic worship without the foundation of unquestioning belief which made the mood possible and genuine. It is unlikely that such a calculated procedure will produce more than a sense of enjoyment; whereas it is reported of a certain Hasidic saint that anyone who saw him dance experienced a powerful impulse to repent of his sins! One can savor the Parthenon, the cathedral of Chartres, or the chanting of Kol Nidre without a trace of pagan, Christian, or Jewish piety. There is all the difference in the world between dedicating the arts to the glory of God—that is, using them for the expression of authentic religious aspiration—and utilizing the poetry of religion in order to produce a reasonable facsimile of religious aspiration.

One cannot condemn those who, unable to make a theistic affirmation with honesty, still attempt to conserve some of the positive values inherent in the life of synagogue and church. But their efforts are not likely to be of much avail unless they lead ultimately to some kind of positive conviction. Appropriately enough, a recent writer on worship concludes his article: "Let us pray—to Someone else, if you please."[38]

But can it be done?

Chapter X

PRAYER

D on't Tell Me What Not to Believe! We have already taken full note of the evils of dogmatism. This lesson seems to have been learned reasonably well by the teachers of organized religion. Those churches which once rejected with indignation and scorn any doctrine but their own are now eager to engage in dialogue with representatives of other persuasions. Whatever motives have led to this change, and whatever we think of the results that have thus far emerged from the dialogue, the procedure itself implies the recognition that those who differ from us are not thereby convicted of guilt, that their views are entitled to a respectful hearing, and that we may even have something to learn from them.

But dogmatism, which for all this has not disappeared completely from churches and synagogues, has other practitioners today. The most notable and ominous are the leaders of the Communist nations—ominous because of the powerful pressures they can exert—who define orthodoxy and condemn heresy with medieval pedantry and more than medieval ruthlessness. As is well known, Communist thought-controls extend not only over philosophic, economic, and political matters, but also over literature, art, music, and even science.

All this, however sinister, is at least understandable as a technique of holding and exercising power. What is harder to comprehend and, in a sense, more culpable is the dogmatism of

Marxian "intellectuals" who live in the free world. Many of those who would jeer at anyone who seriously upheld the divine inspiration of the Bible continue to parrot Marxian doctrine (in Leninist, Stalinist, Maoist, or Trotskyite versions) as self-evident, eternal, and undebatable truth.

A similar array of competing orthodoxies is to be found among the psychologists. "Auld Licht" Freudians continue to dispute with the other analytic schools, much as Calvinists and Arminians did in days gone by. The behaviorists blandly eliminate the data of introspection from the science of psychology; since such data cannot be investigated by behaviorist techniques, they must be treated as nonexistent!

There is, further, a less obvious, but even more widely disseminated and generalized scientific dogmatism. Enormous progress has been made through the adoption of a method which assumes an absolutely continuous, ironclad system of mechanical causation. Too often, however, this assumption is taken to be an account of basic reality; an instrumental device is transformed into a metaphysical dogma. This despite the radical criticism of the concept of causation by Hume—a criticism which Kant could deal with only by treating causation as something in the structure of our minds rather than in the structure of the cosmos. Moreover, this ironclad principle seems to be limited in some measure by the "uncertainty principle" formulated by Werner Heisenberg regarding the behavior of subnuclear particles. Studies in parapsychology likewise suggest the existence of an area where causation does not work in what we consider a normal fashion.

Now many of the latter-day dogmatists, however unlike each other they may be, and however much they may quarrel among themselves, agree on one thing: that religion is not a valid option. Marx's "opiate of the masses" becomes a neurotic illusion in Freud's system—but both rule out religious faith.

Finally, some of those who champion religion in humanist form join the negative chorus especially on the subject of prayer, defining confidently what prayer cannot accomplish.

To all these negative dogmatists, one may rightly reply: Don't tell me what not to believe! I resist any effort to impose a theological doctrine on me because someone else is sure it is true; I rise up equally against those who are sure about what cannot be true. Before a faith is to be ruled out as scientifically untenable, it is necessary for scientists to scrutinize the assumptions on which their own conclusions are based. Arrogance is equally unbecoming to the theologian and the scientist; and it is not characteristic of the greatest, most creative scientific minds.

In the laboratory of one of the great electric companies—so I was told years ago—the research workers used to subject newly recruited colleagues to a mild hazing. The neophyte would be given the project of finding a way to frost an electric light bulb on the inside. After he had struggled with the problem for a while, the others would show him why the undertaking was impossible; they would all have a good laugh then and go on with their serious work. But one young scientist came to that laboratory who had no sense of humor at all. And today electric bulbs are usually frosted on the inside.

● **The Lower Levels.** Most contemporary discussions of prayer deal either with its philosophic and theological propriety or its psychological impact, with prayer theory or prayer experience. But there is at least one other approach—to consider prayer as duty.

Such a notion took a long while to develop. In the Bible, most individuals pray only when they are in need, in time of emergency. In those days the routines of religion were a public matter, and chiefly a system of sacrificial rites. Many of the Psalms were composed as an accompaniment to those rites. Gradually, however, the thought took hold that prayer is important for the individual, even when he hasn't a specific petition to present. We see this development in the personal utterances of Jeremiah, and in certain Psalms which are plainly the utterance of a single individual.[39] Only in the Book of Daniel (composed between 168 and 165 B.C.E., and so the latest work in the Scriptures) do we read of the hero praying three times daily before a window that faces toward Jerusalem (Daniel 6:11). When that was written, the custom of regular prayer at stated intervals was already established among many Jews. From Judaism the practice passed in divergent forms to Christianity and Islam.

At present, this tradition is in disrepair. Not only have many people rejected worship altogether, but many others who believe that prayer is valid and helpful regard it as the expression of a mood rather than the fulfillment of an obligation. They judge the value of prayer by the "lift" it gives them; and they assume that if they don't feel disposed to pray at a particular time, it is better for them to wait till the spirit moves them.

Within limits, this makes sense. The Talmud advises us against praying when our spirit is distracted, and condemns prayer by one who is intoxicated.[40] But it is precisely when we are not in the mood that we most need some devotional exercise. If worship is reserved for those occasions when we feel a strong urge to pray, we may find such occasions becoming more and more rare.

All this applies with special force to public worship—an institution which includes other elements than prayer in the exact sense. Public worship provides a sense of belonging, an escape from loneliness. It often includes the aspect of instruction in the form of reading and exposition of Scripture. If the place of worship is beautiful and the music is good, an aesthetic element is added. But the chief advantage of regular attendance at church or synagogue is that it gives us fixed occasions for contemplating those values which might otherwise be neglected amid the routine and hubbub of daily living.

For worship is, at the minimum, the conscious confrontation of the things we believe in. That may not be prayer in the fullest sense, but in itself it is valid and important. It is the common meeting ground of all who take moral and spiritual values seriously, whether they are unquestioning believers or seekers beset by serious theological problems. Each of us can direct his thoughts regularly to what he does see clearly and hold fast to. If he is not certain (or not yet certain) that he can pray to God, that the traditional forms and practices of prayer are right for him, he can still concentrate his attention and concern on the principles that strongly command his loyalty. Normally we are occupied with specific situations, tasks, desires, and needs. We do what is usual, or what is necessary, or what is convenient, or what is easy and pleasurable. We seldom stop to consider how our actions, decisions, and policies square with the principles we say we believe in. It is therefore necessary, one might say obligatory, at frequent intervals to take a long and loving look at integrity, justice, unselfishness, and compassion, and to judge our own performance in the light of those shining ideals. Such an exercise renews our vision and helps us discipline our lives.

We also need to take time to count our blessings. This likewise does not require a prior solution to all our theological difficulties. We have already discussed at length the problem of evil and suffering which hangs so darkly over religious thought in our time, yet even one who has not come to any conclusion about that problem can still give thought to the benefits and privileges he enjoys. Our nature is such that pain and discomfort rarely escape our attention. We are always ready to complain of what hurts or bothers us. But good health and physical well-being, the ability to breathe easily and move freely, the capacity to see and hear well—such things are ordinarily taken for granted as our right, and many other beauties and joys along with them. To preserve our own spiritual balance, we must spend some time examining the reasons why we should be grateful, even if we are not certain how and to whom the gratitude should be expressed. Thereby we keep ourselves above the level of the beast who eats his fodder with no thought of whence and from whom it comes. (When you come to think of it, there is no more inappropriate figure of speech than that which compares reflective thought to chewing the cud and uses "rumination" as a synonym for meditation.)

Such contemplative worship, which does not include address to the Deity, and which we have designated here as a lower level of devotion, has yet an honorable place within historical religion. In Judaism, the primary place in the daily liturgy is given to the recitation of the *Shema*—the biblical passage which begins, "Hear, O Israel, the Lord our God, the Lord is one" and continues "You shall love the Lord your God with all your heart and soul and might."⁴¹ This passage, to be recited morning and evening, is an affirmation, addressed to the worshiper and not to God. Yet this is the first "prayer" which Jewish children are taught! In the tradition of Judaism, moreover, study is often regarded as a form of worship.⁴²

● **Meditation.**   The devotional activity treated in the preceding section might well be characterized as meditation; it is not quite what we mean by prayer. It is, however, necessary to distinguish meditation as just described from meditation as taught by some of the Far Eastern religions—an exercise that has become rather fashionable in recent years. I am not qualified to assess either the religious or the psychological value of that sort of meditation, and refer to it here only to clarify the difference between the Far Eastern and the biblical tradition.⁴³ Among Jews, and among Christians as well, meditation has generally been understood as meditation *about* something. One might, for instance, ponder the greatness of God revealed in nature, or the divine love as manifested in some event or personality. Or he might engage in self-examination and self-judgment. Or he might simply concentrate his thoughts upon the divine. "The pious men of old," we read, "used to wait quietly for an hour before reciting their prayers, that they might direct their minds to God,"⁴⁴ freed of all distracting thoughts.

But the kind of meditation that has become popular nowadays seems to be an effort to achieve a special kind of consciousness, in which ordinary thought is obliterated. Considerable attention is given to the position of the body during meditation, and in some instances to the control of breathing. Whatever the benefits of such meditation, it appears to be an exercise without conceptual content.

Though these procedures are remote from the normal devotional practices of biblical religion, they need not be ruled out in advance as irreconcilable with Judaism. They are worth thoughtful study. The test of the value of meditation in this sense would seem to be pragmatic. Does the practitioner emerge from meditation with a greater sensitivity to moral challenge and religious duty, with fresh stamina to meet life's responsibilities and challenges? If so, Jewish teachers might well consider borrowing this new resource. In the past Judaism has often adopted and "naturalized" ideas and practices originated by other peoples and sects. If, on the other hand, the effect of such practice is just to make us "feel good," suffused with a kind of pantheistic contentment, and less concerned about the pain and sorrow in the world, we should have to be wary. We might conclude that the Eastern variety of meditation is something like the sauna—harmless if not overdone, but debilitating if carried to excess. No such judgments will be attempted here.

● **The Crucial Word.** When now we turn to prayer as it is ordinarily understood, we at once encounter a crucial word. It is not "God"; that term has been used in such a variety of meanings that even the uncertain, even the skeptic can manage to live with it. The crucial word is "Thou" (or, if you like, "You"). For we usually regard prayer as an address directed to someone. It is an attempt to establish a personal relation with a God we trust in.

This emphasis on the word "You" is not just a matter of grammar. The twenty-third Psalm begins in the third person; but the devout worshiper recites it all as a prayer, hardly noticing the change from "He guideth me" to "Thou art with me." And on the other hand, apostrophe is an age-old device of rhetoric. Wordsworth addressed Duty as "Stern Daughter of the Voice of God," but he didn't really think that Duty is female, or that it will respond to an apostrophe.

There is no need to explain the difference between addressing an abstraction and appealing to someone who hears and responds. Yet even here, one dare not be too dogmatic. One thinks of a Jewish teacher of the last generation for whom the word "God" had only symbolic (or, as he put it, "dramatistic") value; it summed up man's highest aspirations. Yet he used to deliver moving and inspiring prayers, addressed to this symbolic concept! One who was not informed as to his actual views would have assumed from his prayers that he was a convinced theist. Perhaps he was one of those whose inward piety is more intense than their philosophic reasoning would seem to permit.

But however this exceptional individual may have solved his problem, for most of us his solution will not do. If we are going to pray at all, if we are going to say "Thou," it must be to a Being we believe to be real, not to a mere concept of our own.

Modern technology has provided an analogy which many have found helpful in dealing with this subject. Waves constantly radiate from a broadcasting station. They are objectively "there"; but we are not ordinarily aware of them. Only when we tune in do we get sound and even color pictures. Just so, it has been said, God is present and available; but we perceive His presence and help only if we "tune ourselves in."

This analogy suggests (nothing of this sort "proves" anything, it only provides us with a tool for understanding) a way in which we make contact with an objectively real Divinity. In such case, the relationship would be personal on our side only; the viewer may feel that the television personality is speaking directly to him but not the reverse.* Perhaps we can expect no more.

But many continue to hope for and to seek a relationship that is personal in the fullest sense, a two-way relationship—as Martin Buber has taught us to call it, an I-Thou relationship.[45]

● **Communion.**[46]   I have already tried to show that one who is committed to spiritual and ethical values that are more important to him than his own selfish interests has thereby affirmed Transcendence; further, that we cannot wholly avoid ascribing some sort of personality—for want of a better word —to that Transcendence.

Faith may therefore discern in the experience of prayer a communion in which God and man respond to each other.

To one who has had such an experience, the reality of it may be beyond discussion. But the act of faith is still an essential element. Such an assertion is implicit in every account of the I-Thou relationship. What appears to the devout worshiper as a two-way conversation with God might be only a tuning-in on a universal cosmic vibration; or it might be no more than a pleasant self-induced illusion.

---

*Even here we must not be too positive. The human broadcaster may feel the need for a studio audience, and he is eager for postcards and phone calls from his public.

But before we decide which of these interpretations to adopt, we should be on our guard against a widespread prejudice— the prejudice that realism requires us to expect the worst. The happy ending is felt to be less artistic than the tragic denouement; but in life, both of them occur. Many of us have had at one time or another some "lucky break" which no self-respecting literary craftsman would dare to adopt in his story or play. There is danger in wishful thinking, yes; but then we must consider the corresponding danger that pessimism is often self-fulfilling. "If hopes were dupes, fears may be liars." And so if sometimes (here I speak from my own experience) we sense in moments of prayer that God is near us and responds to us, we have a right to trust our own feeling. We need not hesitate to say with the Psalmist, "As for me, nearness to God is good" (Psalm 73:28).

A curious, and in a way reassuring aspect of this subject is what might be called the phenomenon of hostile prayer. It is nothing new; Job protests vehemently to God about the way He runs His world, and later Judaism affords other examples of what has been called "the Promethean element" in prayer.[47] Since the Holocaust, however, it has attained a certain vogue; its best-known practitioner is Elie Wiesel. And stories are told of Jews in the ghettos who formally indicted and convicted God of responsibility for their destruction.

There is no intent here to pass judgment, favorable or otherwise, on this sort of reaction. But its implications are relevant to our study. For one would have thought that anguish over the apparent injustice in the world would lead to one of two conclusions: either there is no moral ruler of the universe, or there is a God who is hostile to man. But in both these cases, prayer would seem to have no place. It is silly to address a God whose existence you deny; and it would not only be futile, but demeaning to address a God who is your enemy.

We might, of course, dismiss angry, denunciatory prayer as a mere beating of desperate fists on the locked door of an empty house. But such an explanation would hardly apply to Wiesel, who has been carrying on his feud with God for many years, in carefully executed books. This phenomenon appears, then, to be an expression of faith, strange as the expression may be. Certainly it was so in the case of Job. It is an outcry against the injustice of a Being we still feel must somehow be just. It is a dramatic mixture of faith and bewilderment. In style, it is utterly different from our presentation of the problem; in substance not as different as one might think.

● **Petition.**   A famous saint is reported to have prayed, "I have no wish for Thy Paradise, nor any desire for the world to come, I want Thee and Thee alone."[48] This may be the way of saints; but ordinary folk have not been shy about asking God for benefits, including material benefits, or about praying for protection against physical as well as spiritual evils. Prayer is ordinarily understood not only as prayer to Someone but as prayer for something.

This of course is the most difficult and painful part of the subject. And what is most difficult is not the scientific argument that petition is of no value—that prayer for a pneumonia patient will not help him to recover, whereas an injection of the proper antibiotic will do the trick without any prayer. For though experience generally supports this argument, we still cannot be dogmatically certain about what prayer can or cannot accomplish.

The moral and religious difficulties inherent in petitionary prayer are even greater. One is illustrated by the familiar example of two warring nations each praying to the same God for support in the project of defeating and destroying the other. Beyond this clash of selfish interests, there is perhaps a deeper difficulty. Is it right to employ prayer for anything else but prayer itself? When we ask for some material blessing, are we not profaning our devotions?

The answer is that to refrain from petition when our minds are preoccupied by immediate and urgent need would be unduly self-conscious, perhaps not quite honest. If prayer means to pour out our hearts before God, how can we not speak of what is uppermost in our hearts? We would want our children to speak openly to us, even if we are not willing or able to give them everything they ask us for.

But the difficulties just mentioned do inject a sobering consideration: What may I pray for? The Talmudic sages warned against "vain prayer"—that is, asking for the reversal of something that has already happened.[49]

But we must scrutinize our prayers for more than formal correctness. Dare we utter a petition that is basically selfish and immoral? We have already mentioned the impropriety of prayers for victory, for someone else's misfortune. And it also seems unsuitable to pray about trivial concerns.

Indeed, prayer offers us a side benefit of great importance: it helps us achieve perspective and a firmer grasp of values. When we become disturbed, unhappy, greedy, or angry, we may well ask ourselves, "Is this issue something to pray about?" In the light of that question, many small things that upset us will appear in proper proportion. Our notion of what we should and should not make the subject of prayer will change as we mature. The child to whom a hoped-for bicycle or doll is the most important thing in the world this week, the adolescent who feels she "will die" if the boy she adores does not ask her for a date, may well pray about these crucial concerns. There is no firmer evidence that we are grown up than a sound understanding of what to pray for.

Perhaps the last word on petitionary prayer was spoken nine centuries ago: "Thou knowest what is for my good. If I recite my wants, it is not to remind Thee of them, but only that I may better understand how great is my dependence on Thee. If, then, I ask for things that are not for my well-being, it is because I am ignorant; Thy choice is better than mine, and I submit myself to Thine unalterable decrees and Thy supreme direction."[50]

AFTERWORD ==========

This book, offering an approach to religious thinking in general, and Jewish religious thinking in particular, illustrates that approach by a reasonably full discussion of some key issues. But in view of its avowedly unsystematic character, I felt no need to discuss all the questions usually included in standard works of theology. Where I felt I had nothing new to say (at least in manner, for I make no claims to basic originality), I preferred to save the reader's time and my own. Thus I have touched only incidentally on such questions as the unity of God, the concept of creation, and the nature of man.

More serious, perhaps, is the absence of any treatment of revelation. I discussed that subject some years ago in "Torah as God's Revelation to Israel" (in *Great Jewish Ideas*, edited by Abraham E. Millgram for the B'nai B'rith, 1964). This essay presented the notion of "progressive revelation" held by many religious liberals, in particular the spokesmen of Reform Judaism. According to this view, revelation is a continuing process, rather than an event (or series of events) in the past. My article explained the idea and its implications, and also pointed out some of the difficulties it involves. More recently, these difficulties and certain others have given me increasing trouble. If, for instance, we recognize the teachings of all wise and good men as part of God's revelation to mankind, how shall we deal with opposing religious outlooks? The difficulty is perhaps manageable regarding disagreements between Judaism on one hand, and Christianity and Islam on the other. Since the latter religions are both rooted in the Hebrew scriptures, we might test their innovations against the biblical norms and ask: Is this or that teaching a legitimate inference from, or extension of, or improvement upon, the "Hebraic truth," or does it distort or negate the earlier doctrine? But we must also consider the great religions of the Far East, which have no connection with the Bible and its outlook. Are the Upanishads and the Buddhist canon as much inspired as the prophets? If so, how shall we assess the life-renouncing doctrine of the Buddha, as against the vigorous affirmation of life expressed in the Bible?

More and more, too, it seems to me that in restudying the Bible, especially the prophets, I have a sense that something special happened in their case, which is not adequately accounted for by reference to poetic or artistic inspiration. But while I am not fully at ease with the usual doctrine of progressive revelation, I have not been able to improve on it.

Two areas of belief remain, concerning which Jewish thought, in the past and the present, displays astonishing variety—the Messiah and messianic age, and personal immortality. On these subjects even orthodox tradition tolerates widely differing views. Here certainly, each reader has the right to apply for himself that "exploratory" approach I have advocated.

Regarding the future of mankind, one can find ample warrant in ancient and modern sources for expecting apocalyptic catastrophe, or a gradual and progressive ascent toward the ideals of justice and peace, or the attainment of an earthly paradise through some kind of natural or supernatural revolution—with or without a personal Messiah. Regarding the future of the individual, there are classic Jewish sources for the belief in a shadowy survival in Hades (*Sheol*), in bodily resurrection, in spiritual immortality, in heaven and hell, and in reincarnation.

But here I want to add a note. The subject of immortality has been explored imaginatively by poets, rationally by philosophers, and more or less scientifically by practitioners of "psychic research." None of these approaches can really be considered religious. A religious faith in immortality, it seems to me, is simply the faith (see p. 40) "that the good and wise God has His adequate solution of evil and suffering"—of all the frustrations and disappointments, all the wasted and ruined lives. What that solution is, the religious believer does not need or aspired to know.

This small book has had a rather long prehistory. Some of the ideas it contains were first presented publicly to a group of colleagues in 1961, and were later worked up into a lecture delivered at the Liberal Jewish Synagogue in London, as the 1971 Claude G. Montefiore Memorial Lecture. After the entire book was completed, it was read by my friends Dr. Sidney L. Regner and Rabbi Harvey M. Tattelbaum, whose helpful suggestions I acknowledge with thanks. Later it was subjected to the critical scrutiny of Jacob Behrman, Seymour Rossel, and Neal Kozodoy, all of whom gave me valuable and sympathetic help in giving the presentation clearer focus. Mr. Kozodoy did much editorial work on the manuscript, for which I am most grateful. The final result is my own responsibility.

Quotations from the Bible are all taken from the new translation being published by the Jewish Publication Society of America, an undertaking in which I was privileged to share. For two instances in which I have ventured to dissent from the published text, see notes 6 and 13.

Chapter VIII, in slightly different form, appeared in *A Rational Faith: A Festschrift in Honor of Rabbi Levi A. Olan*, New York, Ktav Publishing Co., 1977.

My wife typed the manuscript, but that is the smallest part of my indebtedness to her—an indebtedness that cannot even be expressed, let alone repaid—in words.

B.J.B.

NOTES

1. Harry A. Wolfson's *Philo* (Cambridge: Harvard University Press, 1948), argues, against the general scholarly consensus, that Philo, the Alexandrian Jewish thinker of the first century C.E., had a complete philosophic-theological system. Without assessing the correctness of this contention, we note three unquestioned facts: (1) Philo never wrote an ordered presentation of a system; Wolfson pieced the alleged system together from statements scattered throughout Philo's voluminous writings. (2) If there was such a system, no one recognized it as such prior to Wolfson. (3) Philo had no direct influence on the development of Jewish thought, and his indirect influence began to appear only about the time of Saadia.

2. Douglas C. Macintosh, *Theology as an Empirical Science* (New York: Macmillan Co., 1919).

3. Walter Kaufmann, *Critique of Religion and Philosophy* (New York: Anchor Books, 1961), pp. 9 ff.

4. For an interpretation of Job, see the end of Chapter IV.

5. James B. Pritchard, *Ancient Near Eastern Texts* (Princeton, N.J.: Princeton University Press, 1950), p. 207d.

6. I take issue here with note f. appended to this verse in the new Jewish translation. I understand the phrase here in the light of Psalm 23:3, where "for His name's sake" can only mean "for His own sake," i.e., because that is His nature. It has nothing to do with His reputation.

7. Kethuvoth 75a ff.

8. Solomon Schechter, *Some Aspects of Rabbinic Theology* (New York: Macmillan Co., 1909), pp. 13 ff.

9. See previous note and George F. Moore, *Judaism in the First Centuries of the Christian Era* (Cambridge: Harvard University Press, 1927 and 1930).

10. See, e.g., Saul Lieberman, *Greek in Jewish Palestine* and *Hellenism in Jewish Palestine* (New York: Jewish Theological Seminary of America, 1942 and 1950).

11. Akiba's saying is in Mishnah Aboth 3:15; the other citations are from Berachoth 33b and Niddah 16b. See further, Louis Ginzberg, *The Legends of the Jews*, vol. 5 (Philadelphia: Jewish Publication Society of America—hereafter JPS—1925), pp. 75 ff. Ephraim E. Urbach, *The Sages: Their Concepts and Beliefs* Hebrew, (Jerusalem: Magnes Press of the Hebrew University, 1971), pp. 229 ff., holds that Akiba's meaning is simply "All is seen [not foreseen] by God." But the traditional understanding, given in our text, is supported by the following considerations: (1) It accords with the other sayings we quoted. (2) There seems to be no reason for joining the affirmation of free will to the commonplace that God knows all man's actions. (3) The second half of Akiba's saying is a paradox; it is reasonable to assume the same for the first half. Urbach contends that in other Talmudic texts, *tsafui* means "seen," not "foreseen." But other forms of the same verb do appear in the sense of "expect, look forward to."

12. Pesachim 22b, Kiddushin 57a, Bava Kama 41b, Bechoroth 6b. My rendering and explanation accords with that given by Jacob Levy, *Neuhebräiches und Chaldäisches Wörterbuch* (Leipzig: F.A. Brockhaus, 1876), s.v. *derishah* and Marcus Jastrow, *A Dictionary of the Targumim* (New York: G.P. Putnam's Sons, 1903), s.v. *perishah*; and it is compatible with Rashi's comments on Kiddushin and Bava Kama. But in the other two passages, Rashi explains that R. Nehemiah was compelled by logic to reject all his previous interpretations until R. Akiba showed that the principle could be applied to Deuteronomy 10:20 as well. With due respect to Rashi, this seems incorrect. For if Nehemiah had withdrawn all his previous interpretations, there would have been no reason for the question of the students. Moreover,

we should have expected him to say in effect, "Since I
acknowledged my error and desisted, I hope to be rewarded for
my well-intentioned, though erroneous expositions." The
reference to R. Akiba is obviously a later addition. (Cf. the very
different account in Yerushalmi Berachoth 9:7, 14b bottom).

13. The new translation of Jeremiah (Philadelphia: JPS, 1973),
renders the last sentence of this quotation: "That is truly heeding
Me—declares the Lord." Though I prepared the draft text for
the translation committee, I am not entirely happy with this
rendering. The Hebrew root yd^c, as is well known, means not
only "know," but also "care about, give attention to, pay heed
to"; but in the present passage I feel that the sense of cognition
is not altogether absent—though I bowed to the superior
learning of my colleagues. But if the translation I have given
here is philologically questionable, it is certainly a permissible
midrash.

14. Ernest Sutherland Bates, *American Faith* (New York: W.W.
Norton & Co., 1940), p. 210.

15. I found this extraordinary passage in the "The Fatherhood of
God" by George Washington Northrup, *American Journal of
Theology*, vol. 5 (1901), pp. 490 ff. Northrup remarks that
during the nineteenth century, predestinarians evaded the
problem by assuming that all children who died before reaching
the age of reason were among the elect.

16. Morris R. Cohen, *Reason and Nature* (New York: Harcourt
Brace, 1931), p. 165.

17. Berachoth 17a.

18. Shabbath 55a; Genesis Rabba 9.5; and see Solomon Schechter,
Studies in Judaism, first series (Philadelphia: JPS, 1896), pp. 214 ff.

19. James A. Conant, *Baccalaureate Sermon to the Harvard College
Class of 1950* (Cambridge: 1950), pp. 8 ff.

20. Abraham J. Heschel, *Man Is Not Alone* (Philadelphia: JPS,
1951), chapters 1 and 2.

21. Henry Slonimsky, "The Philosophy Implicit in the *Midrash*," *Hebrew Union College Annual*, vol. XXVII, 1956, reprinted in his *Essays* (Chicago: Quadrangle Books, 1967), demonstrates the presence of this notion in traditional Jewish sources and argues for its contemporary value.

22. Claude G. Montefiore, *Outlines of Liberal Judaism* (London: Macmillan and Co., 1923), pp. 70 ff.

23. See, e.g., Mordecai M. Kaplan, *The Meaning of God in Modern Jewish Religion* (New York: Behrman House, 1937), pp. 51 ff.

24. See p. 25.

25. See p. 12.

26. The facts are summarized conveniently in George F. Moore, *History of Religions*, vol. II (New York: Charles Scribner's Sons, 1919), pp. 180 ff., 265 ff.

27. But in 9:7, Amos seems to modify this view: God has indeed shown kindness to Israel, but other peoples have also been guided by His providence.

28. Some scholars, ancient and modern, have explained the "servant of the Lord" differently—as a prophet of the past, as Deutero-Isaiah himself, or as a messianic figure. But such passages as Isaiah 43:10 and 44:1, which explicitly call Israel "God's servant," seem conclusive.

29. For the biblical period see, e.g., Isaiah 56:6-8; Zechariah 8:23. For later developments, see Bernard J. Bamberger, *Proselytism in the Talmudic Period*, 2nd ed. (New York: Ktav Publishing House, 1968).

30. See Casper Levias in *Year Book of the Central Conference of American Rabbis*, vol. IX (1899), p. 180; Abba H. Silver, *ibid.*, vol. XXXVIII (1928), pp. 208 ff.

31. Will Herberg, *Judaism and the Modern Man* (Philadelphia: JPS, 1951), p. 271. On p. 274 he characterizes Israel as "superhistorical."

32. Mordecai M. Kaplan, "Shall We Retain the Doctrine of Israel as a Chosen People?" _The Reconstructionist,_ February 23, 1945. I replied to this article in _The Reconstructionist_ of December 28, 1945, and a rejoinder by Dr. Kaplan followed in the subsequent issue.

33. This broad generalization, naturally, does not fit every case. The book Deuteronomy uses the expressions "to fear God" and "to love God" interchangeably; these expressions do not designate states of feeling, but obedience to the commandments. See Bernard J. Bamberger, "Fear and Love of God in the OT," _Hebrew Union College Annual,_ vol. VI (1929).

34. Joseph Fletcher, _Situation Ethics_ (Philadelphia: Westminster Press, 1966). Fletcher uses the term "love" in the sense of Greek _agape_—an unselfish concern for others; and he insists that justice and love are one and the same thing. But in any case, the decision of what constitutes justice or love in a given situation is left entirely to the gut reaction of the individual.

35. I Kings 8:46; Ecclesiastes 7:20.

36. Kiddushin 40a; contrast Matthew 5:28.

37. Yoma 29a.

38. Edward Graham, "Winds of Liturgical Reform," _Judaism,_ vol. 23, no. 1 (Winter 1974), p. 60.

39. Scholars have frequently discussed the "I" in the Psalms. Sometimes (e.g., Psalms 9 and 129) the nation speaks in the first person singular; sometimes (Psalms 39 and 131) the speaker is clearly an individual. But often (e.g., Psalm 61) the individual identifies himself so completely with his people that the two are inseparable.

40. Mishnah Berachoth 5:1; Bavli Eruvin 64a.

41. Deuteronomy 6:4-9. (Traditionally, the _Shema_ also includes Deuteronomy 11:13-21 and Numbers 15:37-41.

42. Nathan Isaacs, "Study as a Mode of Worship," _The Jewish_

Library, first series, edited by Leo Jung (New York: Macmillan Co., 1928).

43. Of course, exceptions can be found within the vast area of Jewish history. Abraham Abulafia, a thirteenth-century cabalist, taught a system of meditation somewhat similar to that of Yoga. See Gershom G. Scholem, *Major Trends in Jewish Mysticism* (New York: Schocken Books, 1961) p. 139.

44. Mishnah Berachoth 5:1.

45. The terminology of I and Thou was used by a number of Jewish and Christian writers before Buber, but it was he who gave it general currency. Certainly, his book *I and Thou* has had enormous influence on both our language and our thinking.

46. Though often associated with Christian worship, the term "communion" is not out of place in a Jewish context. It is an excellent rendering of the Hebrew *devekuth*, literally, "clinging" (of the soul to God.)

47. Sheldon H. Blank, "Men Against God—The Promethean Element in Biblical Prayer," *Journal of Biblical Literature*, vol. LXII (March 1953).

48. Solomon Schechter, *Studies in Judaism*, second series (Philadelphia: JPS, 1908), p. 181.

49. Mishnah Berachoth 9:3.

50. Bachya ibn Pakuda, *The Duties of the Heart*, gate 8, chapter 3; the passage is said to have been recited by a certain saint after he had completed the regular liturgical prayers.

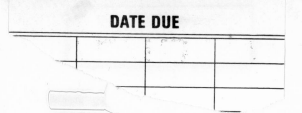

DATE DUE